One Leg and a Cup

One Leg and a Cup

ISBN - 13:978-1976345937
ISBN - 10:1976345936

Credits:

Composition – Terry Celano

Initial Editing – MaryAnn Grembowski

Final editing – Ron Celano
Formatting – Ron Celano

Cover Art – Chris Haponek
Illustrations - Chris Haponek

Website: https://onelegandacup.com/

Disclaimer

Copyright Notice

Acknowledgements

I would like to express my appreciation and gratitude for those that helped make this book a reality. First and foremost, I would like to give thanks to my brother Ron. Completion of this book would not have been possible without his advice, extensive publishing knowledge, and persistent work ethic. To my wife Mary who always supports my sometimes crazy pursuits. To my children, Paul and Ashley, who provided encouragement and help with details such as scheduling, computer accounts, and other tasks. To Vikki Adams and JoAnn Kolbe who stood by, ready to offer legal advice whenever it was needed. Finally, to Jeff Balaka who was the first to proofread the manuscript, providing insight to its flow and readability.

Dear Reader

The stories and interviews herein are about and from panhandlers picked at random. I didn't know what they would say or how they would react. The first few questions for each interview are simple and somewhat redundant. I apologize for that, but the reason for this was to help make the interviewees comfortable and more accepting of the questions that followed. In light of the above, I can assure you that their answers are written as they were told to me to the best of my knowledge and ability. – Terry Celano

Contents

Preface

Have you ever wondered why panhandlers beg for your money? Is that their only source of income? Why can't they go out and get a job like everyone else? Do you judge them by their looks or the clothes they wear?

Over three decades ago I talked to a man who was sitting on a street corner. He was holding a sign in his hand that read, "Homeless." It was strictly curiosity that drove me to strike up a conversation with him. Unfortunately, that conversation led to a short friendship that ended up in a tragedy that will probably haunt me for the rest of my life.

Since then, I have had a hard time donating to panhandlers that populate the streets. Should I make a judgment call and only give to people that look needy or should I help in other ways that would be more comfortable for me? The only way to answer these questions, and many more, was to go out and interact with the homeless in person. Because of the unfortunate circumstances that happened years before, this endeavor would not be easy, but I knew it was time for me to face up to my fears.

I decided to document my findings as part of the healing process and started working out a game plan. That led to one question that could not be answered by talking to the homeless. It could only be answered by me. "What would it be like if I was homeless and had to panhandle on the streets for money?"

This generated several thoughts about how I would handle certain situations. Would I sleep in a park, a shelter or in my car? Would I eat out of a garbage can, eat what people gave me or use my own money to buy food? Where would I go to the bathroom or what would happen if I became sick and needed immediate attention? Last but not least, what if someone tried to rob me? I wouldn't have my phone or a gun. All I would have are the clothes on my back and a sign in my hand. My car would be parked nearby, but fleeing to it would be my last resort. After extensive thought, I chose not to go homeless and hoped to get most of the answers from interviewing panhandlers instead. Nevertheless, to reach closure, I had to at least go out and try begging for myself. The more I thought about it, the more determined I was to get to the answers one way or another.

Introduction

It was the summer of 1985. While taking my normal route through the Detroit area, I was checking out many of the pawn shops, looking for that one sleeper purchase that would keep me going for another week. Business was slow and every day seemed to be a struggle. As a consequence, negative thoughts had been creeping into my mind for some time. It was getting so bad that I started picturing myself homeless and begging for money on the streets.

It was a Thursday morning. That is the day I normally traveled my most dangerous routes. Many of the streets were lined with empty buildings due to the crumbling Detroit economy. It was approaching noon when I drove through a familiar area where there was an obscure pawn shop that I made sure never to miss. Upon arrival, I spotted a handicapped man sitting on the corner adjacent to the shop. He had long hair streaming down to his shoulders and his beard was grey and stringy. It reminded me of an old bird's nest. Through further inspection I noticed that he had one leg, was holding a cup in one hand, and an old cardboard sign in the other that simply read, "Homeless." As I got out of the car, an overwhelming urge came over me to ask the man about his life story. My heart was pounding as if it was going to beat right out of my chest. I approached from behind and tapped him on the shoulder to get his attention. He turned toward me abruptly with a startled look in his eyes that reminded me of a deer staring into a pair of headlights. Slowly reaching out my hand, I introduced myself in a way that would calm his nerves. The gentleman shook my hand with hesitation and after some small talk, I politely asked, "How did you end up in this situation?"

Without delay he began to speak. "I wasn't always like this you know. My life was good growing up. Then at the age of 24, I married a beautiful woman and got a job as a tool and die man in the automotive business," he continued with a sigh, "but then it happened. I started drinking with my co-workers. At first it was just weekends, but then it got to be every day." I then asked, "When did you realize drinking was becoming a problem?" He replied, "It was when I started making alcohol a priority over my everyday life. After four years of marriage, we had a boy and then two years after that a baby girl." His voice started to crackle as he continued, "As time went on, things got worse and I lost everything. I lost my house, my wife, and even my children." At this point I noticed his eyes starting to well up with tears. "Then my health started going south. I didn't take very good care of myself and finally diabetes took one of my legs." I asked him if he was really homeless or just panhandling for extra money. He told me that he was living in a friend's large tool shed with just a heater, a cot, and a port-a-potty.

Asking how old he was, the man replied, "I'm 66 but I feel like 90." Thinking that he probably worked long enough to collect Social Security, I asked if he was receiving any benefits. With a puzzled look on his face, he said, "No, I'm not." I explained that he might be eligible for a monthly check, and with my assistance we could get the process started. The man understood and enthusiastically agreed to receive my help. Before going into the pawn shop, I asked if he would be kind enough to answer one more question. "Sure I will," he replied. With a big smile, I inquired, "If you could have one wish in the world what would it be?" Without taking a breath, he said, "All I want is to be able to have a real drink at a bar with some friends." Confused, I asked, "What is a real drink?" He looked at me as if I should know the answer. "It's being able to just drink a fine glass of bourbon. I'm tired of drinking cheap wine."

After our discussion, I walked into the pawn shop. The owner [Mark] greeted me at the door and I proceeded to tell him about the conversation between myself and the homeless man who sat on the corner outside his shop. Mark said he always had empathy for the old man, but could never get up enough nerve to start a conversation. After conveying his life story, I mentioned that the guy wasn't collecting Social Security. Mark volunteered to help the man get his papers. He also told me that there was a vacant apartment attached to the back of his store. Expressing interest he said, "You know what? The man can use it rent free." After leaving the shop, I started feeling much better.

Two weeks went by before I was able to head back to the pawn shop. Pulling up to the store, I observed that the corner where the homeless man usually sat was vacant. When I entered the shop, Mark greeted me as always. He explained that everything was in order with the Social Security papers. He then said, "It's just a matter of time before the first check arrives. In the meantime, I gave the guy a few dollars to hold him over."

The next day, I had to leave town for a couple of weeks. While away, I was bragging to some friends about how this pawn shop owner and I managed to get a homeless man off the streets. I couldn't wait to get back and see how the old guy was doing.

Unfortunately, I didn't get back to the pawn shop right away due to other obligations. Close to six weeks went by before returning. I was eager to talk with the owner to see if our mission was accomplished. After entering the store, I wondered why Mark didn't give me his usual greeting at the front door. There was this eerie dead silence that wasn't normal. So, I went searching and found him in the back of the shop, sitting on a chair, leaning against the wall. He took one look at me and lowered his head. Wondering what was wrong I asked, "What happened?" Reluctantly, he explained that the homeless man received his first check and within three days drank himself to death. He was found in the back apartment lying face down in his own vomit. I don't know why, but the first thing that popped into my head was that the man finally got his one wish, "....to just drink a fine glass of bourbon." Little did I imagine that he would end up the way he did. A few days later the guilt started to set in, "Would I ever help another homeless person?" Feeling partly responsible for the old man's death, the thought carried with me week after week, year after year.

Over 30 years had passed and I never forgot about the homeless man at the pawn shop. Ever since that unforgettable incident, my thoughts seemed to be more focused on the homeless. It had come to the point that no matter where I went, they ended up being the topic of conversation. But every time the subject was brought up, someone would say, "They're just going to use the money for alcohol or drugs anyway." or "The beggars have more money than I do."

Curiosity was getting the better of me. Finally, I just had to find out why people become homeless. That's when I had this yearning to write a book. I felt that the best way to attack the subject was to seek out and interview panhandlers. That led to the following questions: "Will these people tell me the truth? Would they even talk to me at all?" To be successful, I had to come up with a way to approach them, gain their confidence, and get honest answers. One day it hit me while sitting in the comfort of my home. There are three pieces of information that I believe the homeless would not want to give up. They would not want to reveal their identity, the name of their corner or the place where they live. So, I chose to explain before each interview that their name and locations would stay private. Also, in return for their story I would pay each of them $100 and take them to a dinner of their choice. I thought by doing it that way there should be no reason for them to lie. All I wanted was their story with no names. I sat down with my laptop computer and started to make a list of questions. They had to be interesting as well as personal.

After some thought about how to document the interviews, I decided to record and subsequently transpose each person's answers word for word. This might offend some readers, but in order to capture the full impact of their stories, I determined that it would be best to write them down exactly as they were told to me. At the beginning of each interview I would explain the rules and tell each person not to hold back on their feelings, "Just tell it like it is." I was now ready to start searching for my first subject.

Lady Fingers

"We think sometimes that poverty is only being hungry, naked and homeless. The poverty of being unwanted, unloved and uncared for is the greatest poverty. We must start in our own homes to remedy this kind of poverty."
Mother Teresa [Catholic saint]

The end of fall had approached and although all the leaves were gone from the trees, it was unusually warm for that time of year. For my first interview, I decided to look for a panhandler on the edge of Detroit next to the affluent suburb of Grosse Pointe. The way I figured it, if you're begging, why not get close to where the money is. Exiting off the I-94 expressway, I noticed a young African American woman sitting on a milk crate. She was holding an old tattered cardboard sign. It was dusk on a Saturday and although my headlights were shining directly on her, she was holding the sign in such a way that it was impossible to read. She seemed to be daydreaming by the blank expression on her face. One could only imagine what was on her mind. Could she be thinking about where her next meal would come from or was she fantasizing about lying on a warm sandy beach without a care in the world.

I parked my car a couple blocks down the street, next to an old abandoned factory. As I walked back to the corner where she sat, I was more concerned about leaving the car unattended than conducting an interview. Since this would be my first attempt, I wanted to make sure not to offend her by using the wrong language. Should I use the word "beggar" instead of "panhandler?" Would it even be correct to use the word "homeless?" It was going to be a trial and error thing, so I decided to play it by ear. Approaching the woman from behind, I cleared my throat in an attempt to get her attention. Using years of sales experience, I put a smile on my face that stretched from ear to ear. She quickly looked over her shoulder without any expression. In a soft voice, I gave my name, the purpose of the visit, and informed her that all personal information would remain confidential. After explaining that in exchange for the interview she would receive $100 and dinner, the woman was more than happy to oblige.

Her appearance seemed unusual for a homeless person. She had on clean clothes, and a coat that looked to be nice and warm without any tears in it. Her hair was nicely kept and she had fingernails that were painted in a deep ocean blue. The only thing that looked out of place was that she was wearing a pair of socks with sandals. The temperature that evening was around 42°F and it was pouring down rain. As we were making final arrangements for the interview, I couldn't help but notice that her feet were strategically cocked back on the edge of a mud puddle making sure they would not slide forward. There was very little room between the curb, her, and the guard rail. I considered that her little space.

We decided to meet the following Thursday at 3:00 p.m., five blocks west of her original corner (well into Detroit). This seemed like a good time because it would still be daylight, making it safer that way. She asked if I would drive her to the restaurant. Since there were no bad vibes, I agreed.

On the day of the interview I drove to the area where we were to meet and realized that, "….we're not in Kansas anymore."[1] My anxiety was starting to explode. The buildings were dilapidated and traffic was sparse. There were very few people walking the streets, which gave me an uneasy feeling. Lady Fingers was waiting patiently when I arrived. She looked to be wearing the same clothes, but the sandals were gone and in their place was a pair of untied lightweight shoes that were made of a blue silky material. Next to her side was a large black suitcase. It was the type that someone might take on a long trip (big and bulky). She asked if I would mind opening the hatchback of my Ford Escape, so that her suitcase could be set inside. Out of curiosity I wanted to ask about its contents, but before the first word came out of my mouth she told me it contained her tools for cosmetology school. I now understood why she had beautiful painted fingernails and well-kept hair. After getting into the car, Lady Fingers noticed that I was staring down at her shoes. She told me about a woman that stopped and handed them to her out the car window. She continued to say that the shoes were two sizes too small and that's why she was wearing them with the laces untied.

As we drove away, I asked what type of food she would like to eat. Since a meal was included with the $100, I was expecting her to say something like "a steak." To my surprise, she asked for soul food. We continued down the road for some time looking for a soul food restaurant, but there were none to be found. She told me that her next choice would be a buffet. Here I'm thinking that she wanted quality and all she was thinking about was quantity. It turned out that there were no buffets in the area either, so I continued to drive for several miles. We eventually ended up at a Ram's Horn restaurant, which mainly serves home cooked meals. After walking in, I asked the waitress for the farthest booth from the front door. The last thing we wanted was to have people listening to our conversation. We sat down and I went over the rules one more time, emphasizing that her personal information would not be used. I also encouraged her to please give the complete truth. She replied that there was no reason to lie, especially since nothing could be linked back to her. I then pulled out a black recorder from my top pocket and proceeded to ask questions.

How old are you?
Thirty-two.

What is your nationality?
African American.

In what religion were you raised?
Jehovah Witness.

Are you still a Jehovah Witness?
I don't follow that religion anymore. I believe in God and Jesus Christ. Most Christian religions are pretty much the same. My mom brought me up in that religion until I was five, but then she died. My dad was not around at that time. He left before I was born.

What did your mother die from?
Uterine cancer.

How old was she?
She was 40. She passed away in 1989.

Who raised you after your mother?
My sister helped raise me. We grew up in three different foster homes until I was 18. (That seemed like a lot of foster homes in 13 years.)

Tell me about your first foster parents?
They were a nice black couple, but they were old. We were with them only two years. The woman died and the man moved away. He couldn't take care of us anymore by himself. From there I went to a Caucasian family, but they were abusers.

How were you abused?
Physically and verbally. It was me and three other girls. I really thought they wanted us, but all they really wanted was the money from the state. They would get drunk all the time and that's when the abuse started. It was mostly the woman that would abuse us. She thought her husband was having an affair and would take it out on me and the others. She would always hit me with her fist or kick me. They would also have

friends over the house while they were drinking. Everyone was so drunk that no one noticed when the men would try to sexually abuse me. At age 10, I knew it was time to get out. I went in front of the court and they finally got me out of there. I was set up with the third set of foster parents. I stayed with them till I was 18.

Earlier you said your father left before you were born. Did you ever meet him?
No, he just disappeared.

What about your grandparents? Where were they?
They had passed before I was born.

What happened after you turned 18?
The state put me in what's called, "self-independent living." Then at age 22, I was completely on my own and there was nothing else they could do for me.

What is "self-independent living?"
That's where the state puts you and another person in a two level house. One lives on the top and the other in the bottom. The state also gives you food and some money to live on.

Are you married?
No.

Do you have any children?
Yes, I have a boy and a girl age five. They are twins. I also have a girl age seven.

Are all three of your children by the same father?
Yes, but he's not around anymore.

Where is he?
He's in another state with his other babies' mother.

Do you receive money from him?
No, he doesn't have a job.

Why did he leave?
I caught him cheating on me. As I was pushing him out the door, he picked up a brick and threw it down and broke my foot. I had to wear a cast and at that time I was pregnant with the twins.

Where did the money come from after he left?
I was working two jobs at the time. I was a waitress at I-Hop and also worked in a casino. I would work at I-Hop at night and the casino in the early morning. After the twins were born, the rest of my time I spent with my kids in a rental house. I felt good about that. It was my first real house that I paid for on my own. My children and I stayed there four years until I lost both my jobs. (Losing both jobs at the same time seemed odd.)

How far did you get in school?
I got my GED [General Educational Development certification] at a later time. I'm not a stupid person, you know. But I decided to get a career for the sake of my children, so I applied for cosmetology school. After four months they called me and said there was an opening.

What time do you go to school?
I go five days a week from 5:00 p.m. to 9:00 p.m.

Where are your children during that time?
They're at day care, which is in the basement of the shelter where we now stay.

Where are the kids during the day?
They're in school. I take several buses every morning to get them there. It takes a total of an hour and 20 minutes. That's keeping in mind that there are transfers involved. Once I drop them off, I take the bus back

to my spot where I panhandle. At the end of the day the shelter people pick up my kids from school and take them back to where we live.

How many people work at the day care shelter?
There are three people that take care of 23 kids.

Do you hear anything bad that comes out of there?
No, they're very good people.

What kind of food do the kids get at the shelter?
On the weekends they give them good food like burritos, chips, juice for lunch, and maybe like spaghetti for dinner.

Do you get paid at cosmetology school?
After a certain time period you do. I've only been there three months, so I'm still a trainee. When I become a senior after a year, I can invite people up to the school and get paid for doing their hair.

How did you start begging on the streets?
One day I noticed this old neighbor of mine. She started to tell me about making easy money standing on the corner panhandling. She even told me one time she did a "three way" with a friend and made extra money that way. I told her, "That's not for me." But then one day, I decided to get myself some cardboard and start begging. The first day I ended up making around 80 to 90 bucks in four hours. Fridays and Saturdays are the best because that's when people get their pay checks. Weekdays are slow. You end up making about half of what you do on the weekends.

How many hours are you usually out there?
I'm there from three to four hours a day. When there are two of us on the same corner, I make the most money. People take the same route every day and if they see the same panhandler over and over, they will most likely give the money to the new person, which would be me.

How long have you been panhandling on this corner?
Ever since I started school. It has been about three months.

How did you feel the first time you went out?
I was very embarrassed. I took my cardboard and used it to cover my face. As I peeked around my sign, people were staring at me. I thought to myself, "What are you looking at? You don't know me." I felt like a girl with no face. All I wanted to do was get up and go. But every time I got up, someone would stop and give me a five dollar bill.

What's the most money you received from one person?
One day a man stopped and gave me three, $100 bills. I didn't go back to that corner for two weeks. I don't go back until I run out of money.

Do you have any bad habits?
I don't do drugs and I don't drink. The only thing I do is smoke cigarettes.

I understand how important your sign must be. What does it read?
"Going thru Hard Times. Need Help. Drug Free." With that sign people are just throwing money at me.

Many signs read, "Will work for food." Do you think most panhandlers would work for food?
Most will not. I had a lady stop one time and ask me if I would help her move. She offered me food and some money. I went with her and helped. I was happy to get whatever she gave me. I needed the money. She was a little white lady and thanked me many times.

Has anyone ever offered you a job?
They give me business cards all the time. When I phone them they never return my call. They're just showing off.

Are you looking for a job now?

Yes, but no one wants to hire me with the hours I can work. I don't have a car and remember I take my kids to school in the morning. Plus, I have cosmetology school in the evening.

Has anyone stopped and asked you to get into their car?

This one man stopped and asked me to give him some head. I told him I'm not that kind of person sir. Even when people are nasty like that, I still try to be respectful. Then after that he said, "Get a job bitch," and pulled off. I thought that was so fucking rude. And then the police drive by and say something jokingly like, "Give me a dollar," and I always give them my middle finger. They then say to me, "Do you want to go to jail?" I always say, "I'm not bothering you, so just leave me alone." Sometimes they make me leave the corner. When that happens, all I do is walk around for about 20 minutes, then return to my spot.

Are there people panhandling who are prostitutes?

Yeah, cars pull up and ask them what they would do for money. The next thing you see is that they're getting in the car. That's why when that man stopped and asked me to give him some head, he asked because everyone else was doing it.

Has anything dangerous ever happen to you while panhandling?

One time a carload of kids drove by and shot us with paint balls. They really hurt, especially when it's cold out. Then about 20 minutes later they came back and this time shot us with BB guns. I'm lucky I didn't lose an eye. We called the police but they didn't do a thing.

Now that winter is coming, what are you planning to do?

I will just have to bundle up. I need the money. I got three babies to take care of. With no help, it's hard.

You can either sit on a corner making $20 an hour or you can go out and get a job. Which do you prefer?

Like I told you before, I'm looking for a job but no one wants to hire me. It doesn't seem like a day goes by where I don't put my application in somewhere. They just won't hire me! It's better to get minimum wage five days a week, then to beg and not know how much money will be coming in at any given time.

I don't get it. Why are there so many help wanted signs around? Aren't they hiring?

It's not me, it's them. I want to work. Just give me a job and I'll show you what I can do. One time I saw a "help wanted" sign and went in to apply for the job. They told me the job had been filled. I asked them why they still had the sign out front. They didn't give me an answer.

Why do you think they didn't hire you?

Maybe because they knew I was homeless or maybe because I'm black. I think that's just wrong when someone won't hire you just because of the color of your skin. Can someone determine how hard they work by the color of their skin?

Do you have skills other than cosmetology?

You show me how to do it and I will do it. I have skills in cleaning and janitorial.

Before I decide to give money to a panhandler, I check out their clothes. Do you think that's the right thing to do?

Everyone has their own situation. Look at me. My shoes look good, but they don't fit. I have a rip in my pants, but you can't see it.

I believe one of the reasons people don't give is because they figure that a street person will use the money for drugs or alcohol. What do you think?

They should think that way, but at the same token it also hurts someone like me. It's really not for the giver to decide. I think people many times judge the wrong way. They think if one person takes drugs, they all take drugs. You can't judge a book by its cover until you open it up and when you open it up, you still have to read it. (She's right about that.) People say the rudest things. This one black lady drove by and couldn't believe I was begging for money. She said, "I know you get a first of the month check from the government." I'm not getting a government check. I'm not mentally slow, you know. One day this man drove by and threw a bucket of cold water on me. People just don't understand.

You sit very close to the curb. Isn't that dangerous?

People like to see how close they can get to me with their car. If it's raining, they try to hit a puddle and splash us. Now there's this one beggar we call "bucket man." He carries a bucket with a letter taped to its side asking for church donations. He doesn't need the money. He always parks his beautiful truck around the corner. His truck is nicer than yours. I believe it's a Cadillac.

Is he really collecting for a church?

No! One day I called the number on the paper and they said, "This is not a charity and we are not a church." That's an awful way to make money, using God's name to scam people. I love God and would never do a thing like that.

Isn't it harder sitting on that corner all day than getting a job?

It is, but most beggars look at it as fast money. Plus you can leave anytime you want. (That's true.)

Has anyone ever stopped and asked you for money?
No, but there's this one man who begs on the corner we call "Dirt." He swings his bucket in front of every car and if they don't give him money, he tells them to suck his dick. No wonder he doesn't collect much. Remember, many people take the same route every day.

Has anyone ever tried to steal your money?
Yeah, this group of guys who were cousins with the bucket man tried to take my money, but I had it stuffed in my sleeve. Since they couldn't find it, instead they decided to steal my shoes.

What was the nicest thing someone ever did for you?
This one lady stopped and asked, "What do you need?" I told her clothes. About an hour later she came back with a huge bag from K Marts. She had everything from bras and blouses to a toothbrush.

Let's get back to your kids. Where do they get their clothes?
Sometimes from church and sometimes from the money I collect on the freeway.

What do you want for your children's future?
I want them all to finish school. I also have an insurance policy on them. It costs me four dollars a month for each child. If something happens to me they will have money to fall back on. It's called Gerber life insurance.[2]

You told me you live in a shelter. What's that like?
Me and my babies are all in one room, but we have to share it with another lady who we don't even know. I believe she's on drugs. The shelter people can put anyone they want with us. The room doesn't have a door and there is one bathroom down at the end of the hall. As you see, it doesn't have much privacy. Also, the shelter only has one TV which is in the main room.

Earlier you told me you lost both jobs before you went into the shelter. How did that happen?

About four months ago I lost my job because my baby girl caught pneumonia and was in the hospital for one week. I had to stay with her. I called in and told them what was going on, but I don't think they believed me. So, I brought in the doctor's paperwork, but they still ended up letting me go.

Have you ever spent time in jail or prison?

I was in jail for a day.

What was that for?

A policeman was messing with me so I mooned him.

If you won the Lotto, what would you do with the money?

I would open up a large apartment building for all the homeless people and only charge them 10 bucks a month for rent. There are people out there who really need it.

Who are the most important people in your life?

My kids.

What drastic measures would you take if things hit the very bottom?

I am a survivor. I believe in doing whatever it takes.

Do you blame anyone because of the situation you're in?

I can't blame my mother. She died when I was young. The only one I have to blame is myself. I do believe God puts us in situations that we can learn from.

Is there one last thing you would like to say before we end our interview?

Yes there is - Judge not, and ye shall not be judged.

It was getting close to 5:00 p.m. and Lady Fingers had to leave for school. She asked if I would drive her to cosmetology class. It was only five minutes away, so I dropped her off and we said goodbye to each other.

As I was driving home, my mind was filled with thoughts. The one thing that hit me was that this woman was homeless because of uncontrollable circumstances. She wasn't a drug user or a prostitute, and she definitely wasn't trying to scam anyone. All Lady Fingers wanted to do was collect enough cash for her and the kids to live on.

The No Show

It was nearing Christmas and while out shopping I noticed a homeless man standing on the exit route of a heavily congested strip mall near my home. He looked to be dressed too warmly for the temperature, which was holding at around 58°F. The heavyset man was wearing dirty, all-grey clothes, and needed a bath. His face had at least two weeks growth and his hair looked like a tangled mop. I walked up, told him about my book, and asked if he would be willing to meet with me for an interview. At first he had a confused look on his face, probably because he didn't know who I was. Then he proceeded to talk in a child-like manner. The guy was trying to convince me that he "really" was homeless. I assured him that there was no ulterior motive other than to gather information for my book. Still acting somewhat confused, he eventually agreed to meet with me at the Big Boy restaurant across the street around 3:00 p.m. on the following Sunday. While we stood there talking, a car stopped and gave him what looked like a full box of doughnuts. He opened the box only to find one, which seemed odd. I said goodbye and reminded him one more time not to forget about our meeting. Walking back to the car, I had to wonder if his child-like demeanor had to do with fear or if he had some type of speech or mental issue.

Sunday came and I arrived at the Big Boy parking lot right on time. After 45 minutes had gone by, he looked like a "no show." I went inside the restaurant, but he wasn't there. I'm not sure what went through his mind. My guess is that he thought I was some kind of a government or law enforcement official like an IRS agent or maybe an undercover cop. It was time to give up and go looking for someone else to interview.

A Dog and His Boy

Three weeks had passed since the "no show." On Monday morning I went to visit my good friend Tudy. We happened to get into a deep conversation about the homeless. I mentioned to him that I was in the process of writing a book on that very subject. He agreed that it was an interesting topic and mentioned that the book should help shed some light on the stigma that surrounds homeless people. Then Tudy told me about a young boy with a dog that he saw panhandling on a corner. I asked him for directions to where they were located. Tudy drew a map and that afternoon I went in search for my next interviewee.

Approaching the intersection indicated on the map, I spotted the boy sitting on a small wooden crate with the dog at his side. He had long jet-black dreadlocks and looked to be of African American decent. I pulled my car into a nearby park and ride that was about 300 yards from where he was sitting. I remembered to keep my smile on and upon reaching him, extended my arm to offer a handshake. Afterwards, I talked about my book and asked if he would be interested in telling me his story. He immediately replied, "What do you get out of it?" I told him that my two brothers are authors and my mother completed an autobiography right before she passed away at the age of 94. So to keep with the family tradition, I decided that it was my turn. As we continued talking, I noticed his dog had a bad limp. The boy saw the concern on my face and told me that his dog was hit by a car just before I arrived. The fur on its paw was completely torn off exposing a patch of bare, bloody skin. I offered to help take the dog to the vet, but he assured me that the paw would be cleaned and bandaged. Once again, I asked if he would meet me for an interview. Taking interest in the dog must have helped gain his trust because he was ready to talk right then and there. But since I did not have my recorder, we arranged to meet at 6:30 p.m. that Saturday. He asked if we could eat at a nearby restaurant that specialized in soup and sandwiches. I agreed to the location and asked if he needed a ride. The boy told me that both he and his dog lived in an old Subaru that was sitting at the park and ride on the hill. He also mentioned that his dog would be all right lying in the back of his car while we ate. I wondered if it would be another no show since he questioned my motives to begin with.

Saturday evening came and I pulled up to the restaurant only to find that it closed at 4:00 p.m. every day. I got out of my car and waited in full view next to the front door of the building. A half-hour passed and I was starting to question why he didn't show up. Did I do something wrong? Maybe he thought it was all too good to be true.

The temperature started dropping drastically, so I got back into my car and drove to the intersection where we first met. The boy, his dog, and car were nowhere in sight. Wanting to give him one more chance, I drove back to the restaurant and was pleasantly surprised to find the boy waiting at the front door. He apologized for being late after which we decided to go to a nearby Applebee's. We sat down at a table far from the front door. I told him not to be shy and order whatever he wanted. The boy ordered a steak and an Arnold Palmer.[3] In fact, by the time the interview was over he ordered four more Arnold Palmers. We started to eat and the interview began.

How old are you?
I'm 21.

What is your nationality?
African American.

Were you raised in any type of religion?
My grandparents were the ones to take me to church. They were
Baptist.

Tell me about your mother and father.
My mother and father were just friends. They never married. One night
they got drunk and that's how I was born. They never lived together.

Who raised you?
My father raised me. My mother was strung out on drugs. She got
hooked on crack and is now HIV positive. My father was a drunk. At
age 10, I left my father and decided to live with my mother. I didn't
stick to her rules, so she put me in juvie. We went to court and the judge
decided that I was incorrigible. My mother told the courts that I
wouldn't go to school and that I was out all hours of the night.

Growing up was there any physical or emotional abuse?
No, there was none of that. But in juvie, I got into a lot of fights.

How far did you get in school?
I graduated from high school. I got my diploma while in juvie. They let
me out on the weekends and that's when I stayed with my grandparents.
They were a big part of my life.

What was the best part of your life growing up?
Early on, it was living with my dad, but eventually I ended up living with
my mother.

Why did you go back to your mother?
Because things weren't going so well. He was losing his job because of drinking.

Were things ever good with your mother?
Not really. Like I said, she was always on drugs.

When you were released from juvie where did you go?
I went back to live with my dad and got a job as a bagger in a grocery store. That lasted for a while until I was fired.

Why were you fired?
Because I was showing inappropriate pictures of my boyfriend to some of the girls at work. (Until this point, I had no idea he was gay.)

So, I take it you're gay. When did you first find out?
I knew it at a very young age. I loved playing with dolls and dressing them in different clothes.

When was your first experience?
My first real experience was at age 12. It happened in juvie with an 18 year old boy. The guy was old enough to go to jail for what he did. He approached me and we did things. Not like all the way, but we made out and stuff. I ended up homeless because I was gay.

I'm not sure I understand.
Recently, I sat down with my father and told him that I was gay. My guess is that he knew it all along. Regardless, he told me I had to leave the house. Now I remember! My first real experience was at elementary school in the bathroom. I guess my feelings went back a long way.

Have you ever dated a girl?
I have no interest in girls. I don't even have friends that are girls. You can't trust them. I communicate with them, but try not to get too close.

Do you have a job?

No. I was working a summer job as a landscaper, but summer's over. I've only been on the street a little over four weeks. When I was kicked out of my dad's house all I had was 20 bucks, my old car, and of course my dog, which means everything to me. Even though he's not a person, he's the closest thing in my life. When I'm out panhandling on the streets, I always make sure my dog eats first.

It seems to me that since you're 21 years old and healthy, you should be able to find a job?

I agree with you. But no one wants to hire me. I have three strikes against me. I'm black, I'm homeless, and I have dreadlocks.

Don't you think those are just excuses?

Maybe so, but as I told you my dog means everything to me. Getting my life started is just about impossible. Let's say I get a job. How am I going to take care of my dog? To rent an apartment you need one month's deposit and you need references. Plus, most places won't even let you have a dog, especially the size of mine. So you see, I'm kind of stuck. People stop and offer me jobs, but when I follow up on them they make some excuse why the job is no longer available. People judge me all the time. They think I'm homeless because of drugs or alcohol.

When you panhandle are the people nice?

Yeah, most of the time. A guy just gave me this brand new jacket I'm wearing. That's good, because it's starting to get cold. But once a man put down his window and yelled, "Get a job nigger." He obviously didn't have the balls to say it to my face. He was driving in the opposite direction.

When is the best time to panhandle for money?

Most of the time. It really doesn't matter. I'm sitting on a million dollar corner.

Since you've been out on the streets, what was the most money you made in one week?

Just so you understand, I'm out on the street from morning till night. I did my best during the week of Christmas. I took in $1,500. (That's a nice chunk of money.)

I don't understand. Wasn't $1,500 enough to get you started in an apartment?

You would think so, but you need to take an average for the month. And besides, I still have to live. I need food, pay off some old traffic tickets, need gas, boots, and I had to get my car fixed. Sure it's a lot of money, but when you try to save, the money just goes.

If you could have any job right now what would it be?

My dream would be to become a Detroit fire fighter. I went down to get a job, but they said there was no money to hire.

What does the sign say that you hold while panhandling?

"My puppy eats first, God Bless." Again, my dog means everything to me. Many times people give me food and blankets for my dog.

Do both you and your dog always sleep in the car?

No, if I collect enough money I get a hotel room for the night. I found a local hotel for $69 a day and they allow dogs in the room. If I can pay for a whole week at one time, it's around $300. If I can pay for a whole month at one time, it's $800. So far, I can't seem to save enough money for a whole month. When I do sleep in my car, I have enough room for my dog to stretch out in the back. He has plenty of warm blankets. Since my car is stuffed, I usually sleep sitting up. I run my car for a while till it gets warm, then I turn it off to save gas.

Do the cops ever give you a hard time?

The state troopers don't like it, but the local police are pretty nice. They even give me money.

Do you know any other panhandlers around the area?
There's a guy down the road who begs and actually lives in a nice house. We got in a confrontation one day because he was trying to take my corner. He begs just to get extra spending money, but I need it to live.

Do you ever give money to the needy?
Sometimes when I get extra, I drive out to the east side and give money to the homeless. Or when people give me extra dog food, I drop some off at the humane society.

How would you like to see your future?
I would like to get back to L.A. and live with my mother, but I just can't seem to get up enough money to take the trip. And if I could, what would happen if my car broke down or what if once I got there my mother wouldn't accept me?

Well, I think we covered it all. Is there anything else you would like to say?
I just want to say once again, people shouldn't judge.

As we walked back to our cars, I asked, "How is your dog's foot?" He opened the hatchback of his car and the dog jumped out. I looked down at the injured paw and it appeared to be healing well.

Thoughts about the first two interviews were stuck in my mind. Surprisingly, both people seemed to be fairly normal. I'm not naïve to think that most homeless people are like that. My next interview may not be so easy. It could be with a drug addict or a prostitute. Only time would tell.

Helter Shelter

"Seven out of ten Americans are one paycheck away from being homeless."
Pras Michel [American rapper]

Another week went by and I opted once again to cruise the borders of Detroit. It was only 10°F that morning which indicated to me that it would take a lot of luck to find anyone panhandling. I drove around for a couple hours and did not see a homeless person anywhere. Realizing that I was in an area where my friend Bill had a barbershop, I elected to stop in and see if he had any ideas. Bill agreed that it would be hard to find anyone standing in the blistering cold, especially with the wind chill factor. Then all of a sudden Bill remembered that there was a soup kitchen behind a church that was only one mile down the road. He continued by saying that the homeless would most likely be there because it was around lunch time. Thanking Bill, I got back in my car and drove to the church.

After entering the parking lot, I went around to the back, parked, and entered the side door. Since it was my first visit to this particular soup kitchen, I wondered what the food would be like. To my surprise, it looked like something you would find at a well-attended buffet. The room was filled with the aromas of turkey, mashed potatoes, and freshly baked cornbread. I sought out the cook and asked if I could speak to the man in charge. He introduced me to the manager who, after explaining my intentions, set me up with a gentleman that had been homeless for over two years. I introduced myself and asked if we could talk. He agreed and we went to a nearby Coney Island restaurant for the interview. As with the other interviewees, we sat at the farthest table from the front door for privacy. The homeless man only ordered black

"

coffee, explaining that he was still full from eating lunch at the soup kitchen. On the other hand, I was starving and told him so. "Oh God," I thought to myself. Maybe "starving" was not the right word to use, especially since I had never been without food for any length of time. I stared at his face waiting for a reaction, but he didn't seem to be offended. Once again the rules were explained not to give names or locations.

Could you please tell me your age?
Fifty.

What is your nationality?
Italian on both sides.

Were you raised in a religion?
Catholic. My parents sent me to Catechism and made sure I went to church every Sunday.

Are your parents still alive?
They both passed away. My father died at 59 and my mother died at 64.

What did they die from?
They both died of lung cancer.

Did they both smoke?
Yes.

Do you smoke?
Sure do.

What do you think this means for your future?
If I had known that I would have lived this long, I would have taken better care of myself. (How many times have I heard that before?)

How far did you get in school?
I made it through 10th grade and then went to work. I got my GED much later.

Any brothers or sisters?
I had seven in all. There were two brothers and five sisters. One sister has passed and one brother died of cancer at age 42. My brother worked at the plant down the road and got cancer from asbestos. He couldn't have regular bowel movements and went into the hospital for exploratory surgery. The doctors said that when they opened him up; his insides didn't even look like organs. They were riddled with asbestos.

Are any of your siblings homeless?
Nope, they all have good homes and good jobs.

After 10th grade where did you work?
I was a roofer. It's what I learned and it is all I know.

Are you now or were you ever married?
No, I had three different girlfriends in my life. I ended up having a baby girl by the middle woman. My daughter is now 20 years old. At this moment she's living with her mother and is seven months pregnant.

Do you get along with your daughter's mother?
No, I don't. It's because her husband likes to stir the shit. He's a telephone tough guy.

You told me you are a roofer. When did things start going bad?
Three years ago I lived in a mobile home. There was a knock on my front door and there stood a man with a badge around his neck. The gentleman said he was there to arrest me for back child support. I explained to him that I wasn't behind on my payments. I also told him that there were times when my daughter's mother would show up at my work site just to get her money on time. The officer said the papers

showed delinquency on the records and that he had to arrest me. The court said that I was over $100,000 in arrears. They also stated that I had to come up with 10% bail money. Since I didn't have it, I went right to jail. After 90 days I went back to the court. They finally got a hold of my daughter's mother and she showed the proof of payments. They dismissed my case and I went back home. At first the courts said it was a felony, but now it's expunged. After 90 days had passed, I owed three months back lot rent and had an eviction notice stuck to my door. When you're in the county jail, it's hard to contact anyone. Since I couldn't come up with the back rent or the mobile home payment, the park sold my home.

At that point I had no place to live, so my neighbor took me in. I got my job back, but still I had no permanent place to hang my hat. As time went on, I had another friend who was having trouble making his rent, so I moved in with him which would help us both. He also lived with his wife and daughter. I found out his wife was a pill popper and that's why they were having a hard time making rent. While living in their house I ended up with a roommate who became my best friend. We shared a room in the back of the house.

Then one day my roommate and I decided to start a business passing out flyers. Every day we would load up the neighborhood kids in a van and they would pass out the papers. Then one day my roommate's father who ran a tire business out of his garage asked if we would take it over. His father was getting old and wanted to pass it to his son. Life was getting good. A few weeks went by and that's when it all happened.

One day my roommate and I were cutting through a parking lot to get a bottle of alcohol at the store. Just then a car drove by and some guy yelled out of the passenger's side, "Get the fuck out of the road." Since we weren't even in a road, my buddy flipped him the bird. I didn't even notice what was going on. This African American guy got out of the car and walked towards my buddy who was just five steps behind me. My roommate turned and started walking back towards the man. Before I knew it, they were standing face to face. The black man pulled out a knife from his jacket and stabbed my friend right in the chest. Then this dude started to come towards me. I pulled out my box cutter and flashed it in front of his face. We got close enough to where I made a decision to rock him with my fist. He then wobbled back to the car and they both took off. My buddy laid there in the parking lot with blood shooting out of his chest. I tried putting pressure on the wound with one hand and calling 911 with the other. Right then two ladies showed up and dialed it for me. At this point I took my box cutter and cut off his shirt. Blood was squirting everywhere and no matter how hard I tried, I couldn't stop the bleeding. Emergency got there pretty fast and they loaded him in the back, but he was DOA at the hospital. It's been two years now and they never caught the two guys. Anyway, since my best friend and business partner was dead, everything went to hell in a hand basket. I couldn't pay my rent and there was no place to go.

I seem to be missing something. You worked all your life and had several businesses. What happened to all your money?
I'm a drunk. For the past 10 years I've drank a fifth of vodka every night. Before that time, I either drank whiskey or tequila. But that type of alcohol makes me very mean. That's why I switched.

When did you start drinking?
When I was 16 years old.

When do you think it started to become a problem?
Right out of the gate. My father would take me to the bar at that age. We were drinking buddies. He was a drunk too. The only time I don't drink is when I'm in jail or the hospital.

Why were you in the hospital?
From drinking, I keep getting pancreatitis. Now that I understand more about the disease, I don't care about the pain in my abdomen. There are no more hospitals for me. I just continue to put up with it.

You told me you're still roofing every once in a while. How can you lay down a straight line of shingles if you're drunk?
As long as there's work, the man will come and pick me up. The whole crew is usually hung over, but it doesn't bother me. I've been drinking so long that I never have time to get sober. In fact, I can lay shingles as straight as an arrow when I'm drunk. But when I get the DTs[4] [Delirium tremens], everything starts to get crooked.

What do you mix with your vodka?
I drink it straight out of the bottle. The longest I ever went without drinking was the 90 days in jail. Rehab just doesn't work for me. As soon as I get out, I go directly to the liquor store. The doctors tell me it's harder to give up liquor than heroin. I never did heroin, but a long time ago I did cocaine.

What type of vodka do you drink?
I like mid-shelf. [There are four tiers - value, middle-shelf, top-shelf, and luxury.] None of that paint remover stuff. It usually takes me about half a gallon to be somewhat out of control. When I go to jail for drunk driving people are amazed how I can act so sober after blowing such a high number. (That's nothing to be proud of.)

Do you attend the church in front of the soup kitchen? And if so, do you pray to God for help?
Yes. I go every Wednesday and Sunday, but I feel God has too much on his plate to take care of someone like me.

Do you feel you're not worth it?
It's not that at all. If anyone is going to help, it has to be me.

Let's get back to when your buddy was murdered. Why did you move out of the house?

Right after my friend was murdered; there was a lot of talk around the neighborhood. People would say that I just left my friend lying there in the parking lot. Even though that wasn't true, I felt it was time for me to move away. So, I picked up and went to live behind a buddy's house in Detroit. He had a mobile pull trailer in the back yard. But later I found out that his wife was a care giver and was growing more marijuana than she should. At that point in my life I didn't need more problems, so I decided it was time for me to get out. From there I moved into a garage. It was owned by the parents of my buddy who was murdered. They offered me his bedroom, but I didn't feel comfortable doing that. His parents loved me to death, but then after a year my friend's parents moved out and they let their grandkids take over. The grandkids told me I could stay in the garage, but I felt it wasn't right. So, at that point I started spending my nights in the local park.

Did the cops ever kick you out of the park?

I always made sure to go way back in the trees. The cops were too lazy to get out of their car and check things out.

It sounds like you go back and forth when it comes to finding a place. Do you think there will be enough money to live in a home once you're old enough to collect Social Security?

I'm fucked. I've never received a paycheck in my life. Everything is under the table. I've never paid a penny to the government. The way I look at it, what can they do to me? I have nothing. If they put me in prison for tax evasion, at least I would have a place to live. (He was right about that.)

I know all your money isn't spent on booze. So, what do you do with the extra?

I go back to where you found me at the soup kitchen and give it to my buddies who are in the same situation.

I told you at the beginning that I'm mainly interviewing people who stand on corners holding signs, panhandling. Have you ever done that?

I would never do that. I would be too ashamed if someone drove by like my family or friends. Once I was walking in Detroit and saw this man begging on a corner. When he was done, I watched him walk back to his Cadillac which was parked at a local gas station. This guy should have had his ass kicked. The next week there he was again on the same corner. I walked up to him and said, "If I catch you out here again you will be homeless and handicapped." Don't get me wrong. There are many people out there who need it. Like this one lady I saw with no legs. Why is it that people who have money take away from those who don't?

What do you do about health care?

I'm on disability because of my bad knees. I have Michigan health care.5 It's the best there is.

Getting back to the soup kitchen. Are the people there mostly alcoholics?

Oh yeah. The kitchen closes at 3:00 p.m. every day. One day I came in 10 minutes before closing. One of the workers told me that there were still some peanut butter and jelly sandwiches in the back. I told her I am not here to eat. I'm just looking for a drinking partner for tonight. You know, no one likes to drink alone.

I noticed that every time you talk about you're drinking, you start to chuckle. Is that just a cover up for your misery?
Yep, that's exactly what it is. When I use to drink that dark liquor, I would never go home without looking for a fight.

I also noticed you're wearing very nice cloths. How can you afford those?
I get them from the church. Look, they're all brand new. Even when I lived in the garage and at the park, the church always made sure to help me. I do like to give back. When trucks pull up to unload, I always try to be there and help.

Well, I believe it's time to wrap this up, but let me ask you two more questions. Who is the most important person in your life and where do find yourself in the future?
The most important person is my daughter. As far as my future goes, I'm looking to get back on point. I am a functioning alcoholic and trying to get back to work. If you need to get a hold of me for any further questions please call on my phone.

I was starting to realize that many people are just handed a raw deal. Here is a guy who probably would have never ended up the way he did if it wasn't for his father. Alcohol is a very strong drug which can control everything you do. Even though I've never had a drinking or drug problem, I can only imagine how tough an addiction would be. Life is not always easy, but it only gets tougher if there is a substance like alcohol controlling it.

Three's Company

It was now late January and I was heading to the Miami Beach antique show which goes on every year at that time. At first I wasn't going to take my recorder, but it dawned on me that warm weather might attract an abundance of homeless people. That led to my next thought, "Would the homeless collect more money where it's cold or where it's warm?" Not only would there be less competition where it is cold, but I believed the "poor me" factor would help them collect larger amounts of money. On the other hand, you have better mobilization where it is warm. A person can panhandle to people driving by as well as pedestrians.

I rented a condo in South Beach right near the convention center. With my recorder in hand, I headed out to find a person to interview. It didn't take long before I came upon three people sitting on a curb (two men and a woman). As I was passing by them, the woman blurted out, "Do you have a buck?" The first thing that came to mind was, "Why only a buck?" I looked down at the three of them and exclaimed, "How about 100 bucks?!" Right away the youngest man started to back off. I'm sure he was wondering why I offered $100 when the woman only asked for a buck. That prompted me to tell them that I writing a book about the homeless. There was some apprehension amongst the group, but I continued by telling them that in addition to the money, they would also receive a lunch. The woman then asked, "Does that mean a drink too?" I replied, "Yes you can have a drink." Well, that got their attention. We walked over to a nearby restaurant and sat down at an outside table.

The waiter wasn't happy with us sitting in his section. Apparently he recognized the homeless people immediately. Right then the manager came out and marched toward our table. I decided to take charge of the situation and after calming him down we began to order. It turned out that only the young man wanted lunch. The other two were just looking for a drink. Come to find out, the restaurant only served beer and did not stock hard liquor. That was fine with me as I flashed back to the ordeal that happened in 1985. The two men were okay with beer, but the woman insisted on vodka. I mentioned that when the interview was over they could take the $100 and do whatever with it. The younger of the two men told the woman to quit bitching, so he could tell his story.

I started by asking all three why they were living on the streets. They did not answer the question, but instead talked about their addictions. The youngest mentioned that he had been off of heroin for three months and now just considered himself an alcoholic. The other two were brother and sister. They also said that they were alcoholics, but did not indulge in hard drugs. The young guy, who didn't trust me at first, seemed to be the most talkative, so I decided to start with him.

While waiting for the food and drinks, the woman removed an old towel from a tattered bag and draped it over her head because she was too hot sitting in the direct sun. After we moved over to a shaded table, I began to interview the young man despite the waiter continuing to show his displeasure.

How old are you?
Thirty.

Tell me about your parents?
My dad died when I was seven years old. At that point my mom and I didn't get along, so I went to live with my aunt and uncle.

How far did you get in school?
I had two years of college. I was raised in Baltimore.

When did things start going bad?

Well the problem started as a baby. My grandma would put whisky in my milk, so I would stop crying. And when I was teething, she would rub it on my gums. Then I started drinking heavy at age 16. I would drink a fifth of bourbon a day. Making it through high school and college was not easy, especially since I was drunk all the time. Then at one point I started using heroin.

Are you using heroin now?

No, like I said, I've been clean for three months. But, I started it in high school with a girlfriend. We tried snorting it a few times and then we quit. After that we decided to have cocaine parties every Friday night. I worked two jobs to help pay for our habit. But as time went on, I became homeless. Eventually I hopped on a train and went to South Carolina where my mother and sister lived. But then my mother said to my sister, "Whatever you do, don't let him move in." So, my boy from prison picked me up. He explained to me that West Palm Beach was the best place to go for rehab. But once we arrived there was nothing for me, so I just ended up getting hooked on roxies.

What are roxies?

You know, Roxy cotton or Percocet 30s. [These drugs are usually used to treat pain]. While on that, one day I ended up going to detox. After getting out, I still had $300 in my pocket. So from there, I went to the train station and purchased a ticket back to Baltimore, but there was a problem. They wouldn't let me on the train because I was intoxicated. Come to find out the ticket was non-refundable. I still had $200 left, so I went to Miami and hooked up with the homeless people. Stayed there awhile, then went back to Baltimore and got a job. Then once again I came back to Miami, but this time with $3,000. From there I hooked up with my boys from downtown and went right back to using heroin.

Are the drug dealers always trying to hook you up?
Hell yes! Once they find out you have money, they follow you around constantly. After getting back to Miami, I decided to meet up with an old friend. He was the first one to shoot me up. After that, I was on heroin for eight months straight. I then ended up in a shelter and OD'd four different times.

How did you stop using heroin?
I found out my body couldn't take it anymore. Having Hep C and cirrhosis of the liver, I figured God only gives you so many chances. I figured my time was up. So, I went and snorted one last uncut bag. I fuckin threw up right away and OD'd. I stopped for a while, but about three months later I ended up trading a submarine sandwich for a bag of heroin. That was the last time.

Do you feel God gave up on you?
God loves everyone, but you have to know your limits. When people hand me money on the streets I always say, "God Bless you." And I don't just say it to say it, I really mean it. I try to pray at least once a week.

Do you ever hold a sign asking for money?
No, it's much easier to just ask straight up. I just say that I need money for alcohol, food or for a blunt wrap. [A hollowed out cigar filled with marijuana.] If I just tell the truth I get more money.

Have you ever gone to prison?
Yeah, I kicked a cop.

Tell me the story.
I was sitting at a bench waiting for the bus. A cop came by and asked for my ID. He pulled an empty beer bottle out of the trash and said I was drinking in public. I told him that I don't even drink beer, only vodka. At that point he threw my wallet in the trash. I then called him a

nigger and he threw me down to the ground. That's when I kicked him in the leg. They wrote me up for open intoxication and two "resistances" without violence. Because of my past record they wanted to give me a year, but I got it down to six months.

What was your prior for?
Two gun charges. My brother and I were pulled over. He had guns in the car and I took the rap because he was going to college. I ended up doing two years.

What would you consider the worst thing you ever did to get money for heroin?
I'm not proud of it, but I let a man suck my dick. I'm just being honest. You know honesty is the best policy.

Did you ever do a robbery?
I did a lot of strong arm and beach robberies.

What exactly is a strong arm robbery?
It's when you strong arm someone and take their money. I would come up behind and choke them out.

Looking back, how do you feel about hurting those people?
One thing I can say is that I've never wronged my family. You do what you got to do to survive. Hey, if I'm hungry, shaky or sick, I need to find a way to get some money. Everyone out here is fair game. Just last week I passed out from drinking and someone took $35 from my pocket. It's a dog eat dog world. My friend and I used to rob beer trucks. One day we robbed a hotel out of $8,000 of liquor. We got caught and my boy did one year for me. At that time, I was only using alcohol. With all the drinking, I would throw up at least three times a day. I did whatever I had to do not to get sick. One thing I can say that I've never done and that's poop my pants. I can't say that for my two friends. (That was a strange change of thoughts.)

When was the last time you strong armed someone?
It's been about a year. I stopped right after my niece was born. I don't want her to see me as a bad person. Don't get me wrong, I have stolen bags right off the beach, but the only people I would strong arm are the ones who would do the same to me. We know who they are.

So, let me get this straight. If I was out at night walking alone in a dark area, you wouldn't strong arm me?
No, I wouldn't. Again, it's only the type of people who would do it to me. First of all, you have to live on the streets to really know what life's all about. Then you will see people's true colors. How they work and who gives back. You should live on the street at least one year. You will know who's cool and who's not. You have categories. You have junkies, Meth heads, and you have alcoholics. The alcoholics are actually the best people to hang out with.

If you have to use the toilet where do you go?
Dressed the way that I do, it's not easy. If I'm near a restaurant I have to tip the waiter to use the bathroom. Sometimes I go in the bushes and sometimes at the beach. One good thing about living in South Beach, if I have to clean up, I just go to the beach showers. Sometimes we hotel hop and get a free breakfast. We also use the hot tub and pools.

I noticed that you have a scar across your chest. How did that happen?
I guess you would not have noticed that if I was wearing a shirt. One day I saw my boy walking down the beach. He was very drunk. I went to give him a hug and he thought I was going to strong arm him. He pulled out a wine cork screw and cut me.

You keep saying, "my boy." What does that mean?
My boy means my friend.

Did you get stitches?

I get stitches all the time. I'm constantly getting in fights. Look, I've broke every bone in my hands.

Would you consider yourself a mean drunk?

No, not at all. Someone would have to be talking shit to me in order to fight. We hang out in groups. In our group we watch each other's back. If you're in a group of three, two of you sleep, and the other one stays awake.

How long can you go without alcohol - about two days?

No, I can only go around six hours. After that I will die.

How much money do you collect in a day?

On an average, each of us makes about $60.

What happens if you get sick? Do you go to the hospital?

No, just last week I was bleeding from my nose and mouth. A tourist called an ambulance and watched me until I was loaded into the back. Then the driver drove me a few blocks away and kicked me out. I'm a diabetic too, but no one cares.

How are you going to get out of this mess you're in?

I will just have to sober up and try to get a job back in Baltimore.

Are you drunk right at this moment?

You better believe I am. You would know if I wasn't. I would be very sick.

When I first walked up to you, I felt you didn't trust me.

You're right. I've been screwed so many times. When I was young, I was abandoned by my parents. It's hard to trust anyone, but I can tell you this - out here I can do what I want to do.

Getting back to what you said earlier about not carrying a sign. If you had to carry a sign, what would it say?
"I need money for booze." That way they know I'm not a liar. When people do give us money they only say one thing, "Please don't use it for drugs."

I know I'm jumping around with my questions, but thoughts just keep popping up in my mind. What happens when you need a haircut?
I either get my hair cut in jail or I have a guy who cuts my hair in a john for a four pack. Sometimes I go down to the beauty school and get it cut for five bucks.

Why don't you sleep in shelters?
Because they're all downtown. And besides, there all full of crack-heads.

Do many of your friends die on the streets?
You hear that they die all the time. They die from an overdose or they may die from a "hot shot."

What's a "hot shot?"
That's where a dealer adds a substance into the heroin that can kill you. Many times the dealers do it on purpose. They usually do it when you have a bad debt. Some dealers cut it with almost anything, but most dealers usually like to cut it with B12 or Fentanyl.[6] In fact, a lot of street people like to get high on Fentanyl patches. You can make it into a powder form or it can be liquefied. From there you can shoot it right into your veins.

Where on your body did you usually shoot up?
At first, I started with my hands. I didn't want to look like a junkie. But all those veins dried up, so I started using my legs. When I got heavily involved, I began to use my arms.

I notice you have some bad sores on your arm. Is that caused from drugs?
No, it's not. I was drunk a few nights ago and I tripped on the cement. Welcome to the homeless. You know the main reason I'm down here? I want to stay away from my family. Because of my alcoholism, I always give them a hard time. They love me to death, and that's why I don't want to give them anymore heartache.

(I decided to move on to the brother and sister. My first question was to the brother.)

Your sister seems pretty drunk. Is she on alcohol and drugs?
She's just a little retarded. She only drinks.

How old are the both of you?
I'm 51 and my sister is 48. Actually, my sister and I were business partners for about 30 years. We had a falling out and split up for a while. We are originally from New Jersey. We came down here not because we were homeless, but because it's warm.

What did you do for work?
I did plumbing with some heating and cooling.

Why don't you work now?
I'm disabled from drinking. I have pancreatitis and cirrhosis.

Do you collect disability?
Yes, around $1800 a month.

Can't you live on that?
No, because I have to pay child support and I need money for medicines. But here is where the main problem started. When my sister and I got down here, within two hours we were robbed of everything. They got our luggage, wallet, and our ID. Without all that, I can't go anywhere. All I can do is hop on a bus and go back to Jersey. Back

home I own two homes outright and collect rent on both of them. My other sister puts the money in the bank for me to help pay my child support. So until we get back, we're living on the streets.

When did your sister start drinking?
She started at age nine. Our family was on a boat one day and my dad cracked open a beer. He gave it to her and that's all it took. We're not drug addicts you know? We just stay quiet and try to maintain. As I look back, we had a pretty good upbringing. My mother and father always made sure that I had enough chores to keep me busy. But I do remember one time, I got in trouble and my parents made me sleep in the back yard. We had to learn how to watch our tongue.

I know your sister's drunk, but how about you?
Yeah, I have a buzz right now. I have to drink every day. It takes me at least a fifth to feel good. As you see, I'm completely coherent and calm. The longest I have gone without drinking in the past 30 years is four months. Now my sister, on the other hand, will not drink when we go back to Jersey. She only stays drunk down here. The reason we originally came down here is because our bodies were hurting. Up north, in the winter, it only stays around 20°F. We're getting old you know?

Were you ever married? I see a woman's name tattooed on your neck.
Yes, I was married twice, but here is the weird thing. They both had the same first name. The cool thing is, I didn't have to change my tattoo.

Did your drinking have anything to do with your two divorces?
No, I never drank in front of them. They were just plain liars. We never agreed on anything. If I said up, they would say down. If I said left, they would say right.

Do either you or your sister have phones?
I had a phone but the other day my sister broke it over someone's head.
Now I'm trying to get it replaced.

Do you have a driver's license?
I did, but I've lost it so many times, I'm not sure if I'll ever get it back. I
have been arrested 24 times. I would mainly get arrested because of
COLA. Do you know what COLA is? It's cost of living adjustment.
Most of the time I didn't make the full child support. They would send
the paperwork to the wrong address. So every time I went to make a
payment, they told me I was not paid up to date. And when that
happened, they would take me away. What else could I do?

How do you travel around?
We walk or take the bus. That's all we can do right now.

**When asking for money, what's the worst thing someone ever said
to you?**
They say things like, "You piece of shit, you looser, fuck you, get a job."
But you know what? This is still the best place to live when you're
homeless. It's like an outside mental hospital. Just on this street alone
there are about 80 homeless people.

Do you have health insurance?
Yes I do, but it does me no good. Down here they just kick you out
right away.

Why do they do that?
It's because I go in too many times. Just the other day I was so weak
and dizzy that I had to go to the hospital. They kicked me out at 3:00
a.m. without even a bus pass. I had a five mile walk back and was
getting dehydrated. You can't drink out of someone's fountain or you'll

just end up in the police station. So about every mile, I would have to stop and get my composure.

Right now it's 1:00 p.m. When was the last time you had a drink?
I woke up this morning and started with a pint of vodka. The last time I saw the doctor he told me that if I am going to drink, then I need to drink dark liquor. It's better for me. (I had to wonder if he was being facetious.)

How would you like to see yourself in the future?
I know it's too late to stop drinking, but the one thing I would like is for my sister and me to go back home and live a somewhat normal life.

At this point, the interview was starting to fade, so I thanked the three and went on my way.

Thalidomide Phenomenon

"There is much suffering in the world - physical, material, mental. The suffering of some can be blamed on the greed of others. The material and physical suffering is suffering from hunger, from homelessness, from all kinds of diseases. But the greatest suffering is being lonely, feeling unloved, having no one. I have come more and more to realize that it is being unwanted that is the worst disease that any human being can ever experience."
Mother Teresa (1910-1998) [Catholic saint]

Earlier that same morning I briefly talked to a man who had deformed arms and hands, and did paintings with his feet. I told him about my book and asked if he would give me an interview. At first he talked a lot of mumbo jumbo, but then after about 10 minutes he settled down and his sentences started to make some sense. We agreed to meet at 2:00 p.m. that afternoon.

Almost an hour had passed since the last interview and I wanted to make sure not to miss my afternoon appointment. So, I hurriedly went back to where the street artist was sitting, but he was not there. I then started walking up and down the streets looking for him. After a good 45 minutes I was just about ready to give up and there he was, propped up against a yellow stucco wall at an old church. I walked up to him and asked if he remembered our conversation from that morning. He didn't give me a direct answer, so I gave him my pitch all over again. The man finally understood and agreed to the interview. Feeling at ease, I sat next to him and started asking questions.

I see you are handicapped. Can you share with me what caused it?
I was a Thalidomide[7] baby. In the 1970's, I was born in Alabama. My mother was taking the drug Thalidomide to help her with morning

sickness. Mothers who took that drug ended up having their babies born with no arms or no legs. I consider myself lucky. I have hands and my legs and feet are fine. It only affected my arms.

How old are you?
I'm not sure; I was born in the early 70s.

Is your mother or father alive?
My father is fast asleep. He's lying in those bushes over by the fountain.

You mean to tell me your father is homeless too?
He sure is. Do you know, he's a war vet? (I would have liked to interviewed his father, but I wasn't about to wake him up.)

Where is your mother?
I'm not sure. I was with the both of them till ninth grade.

Were you enrolled in a special school?
Yes I was. After quitting ninth grade, I started selling Columbian Gold. [A strain of marijuana.]

How long have you been on the streets?
Around seven years now.

I see you're next to a church. Do you follow any religion?
None.

Do you believe in God?
I sure do. Look at my pictures that I draw; each one shows the eyes of God.

Your pictures are very colorful. How long do they take to complete and what do you sell them for?
As you see, I don't use paints. It's much easier with colored pens. Each picture takes me about one week and I charge $60.

Sixty dollars isn't much for a week's work. Is that all you live on?
If I just had to live on my drawings, it wouldn't be enough. I do have this cup next to me. People will walk by and give money.

I don't know if you remember from our conversation this morning, but I'm paying you $100 for your story. Is that okay?
I don't want it and I don't need it. I have $1,400 in the bank.

I know you're asking $60 for your drawings, but can I pay you $100 instead?
(I had to figure a way that he would take my money without being offended) That would be okay. Did you notice when you turn the picture upside down, it shows a different face?

I did notice that. I also noticed that you have a pretty steady foot. Is that the only way you draw?
I'm right footed and right handed. Even though I only have hands coming out from my little arms, if I stand at a table and lean over, I can

draw that way too. I have to tell you a story. One day a guy tried to rob me as I was sitting down. He grabbed me by my one leg and dragged me half way down the block. I have very strong legs you know. With my free leg I kicked him so hard; he was lifted right off his feet. They had to take him away in an ambulance. I ended up with a bloody chin and my balls were killing me, but I was the winner. My balls hurt so bad. That's one time I wouldn't have minded if I was born a woman.

I see a beer sitting next to you. Would you consider yourself an alcoholic?
Yeah, I like my beer. In fact, there's another right over there behind my picture. I'm also a pot head. A little pot doesn't hurt every once in a while.

Earlier you mentioned that you had a bank account. How do you have an account without a permanent address?
They all know me by my face. They won't do any transactions if I'm not there. Believe it or not, there's a guy who comes in the bank who almost looks exactly like me, but, he has all his arms and legs. Oh look! Over there! See the old guy with the gray beard? That's my old man. At least I think he's my old man. Maybe that's a dog, I don't know. (He's starting not to make sense.)

How long have you been drawing?
Ever since I was a kid.

Do you know if any of your pictures are in art galleries?
Maybe, I believe there is one of my pictures in every country of the world.

Do you paint pictures other than the eyes of God?
No, I don't think so. I like to do the eyes. It always helps remind me of God's blessings.

Do you sign all your pictures?
I try to, but every once in a while, I seem to forget.

Hate to change the subject, but where do you go to the bathroom?
In the bushes.

Sorry I'm asking this next question, but I'm very curious. When you go number two, how do you wipe? (I can't believe I asked that!)
See the paper in my top pocket? I pull it out with my mouth and drop it on the ground. When I'm done, I sit on it and scoot like a dog.

Where do you sleep?
Right around the corner in the bushes. Did you know Maria used to wipe my butt?

Who's Maria?
You know, Maria -----.

You mean to tell me the famous Maria ----- used to wipe your butt?
Yep, that's right. And not too many people know this, but she also had my baby. I think it's a boy. I'm not sure, but I think I have three kids in all. I'm a pot head, weed-weed-weed. (He's losing it again.)

When I met you this morning, you were really wound up. Were you on something?
I sure was - strong coffee.

The homeless people around here say that they stay in groups for safety reasons. Do you have a group?
No, I stay all to myself. I don't trust anyone around here. If I have to go to the store for something, I take my bag of weed with me. That way I know it won't be stolen. As for the other stuff, I get tired of carrying it all the time. Most people around here know that all this junk is mine, so they won't touch it. But if I left my weed lying around it would be gone.

Can you legally smoke marijuana?
I went to court the other day and the judge fined me for drinking in public, but threw my marijuana charge out. They did take my weed away from me.

Did you ever have a job?
I use to drive a white van and cut grass in the woods. I would lean over on the steering wheel of the lawn mower with my chest and move the top half of my body back and forth to maneuver around. In the back of the van I would have a lawn mower and trimmer. I don't think people like me. I don't think God likes me. I'm schizophrenic you know.

Don't you think God has a special place for you in heaven?
I don't know. I'm psychotic.

(After asking the last question, he stood up and started walking away with tears streaming down his cheeks.)

Where are you going?
I gotta pee. Watch my stuff.

(Ten minutes went by and I had to wonder if he was ever going to return. He finally came back and sat down against the church wall.)

You've been gone for quite a while. Is everything okay?
Yeah.

Do you name your paintings?
No.

You seem to have quieted down since you got back. And now I see you're starting to get a little emotional. Are you sure you're okay?

There was no answer. It was like he just clammed up. After expressing that we had a nice talk, I had a somewhat guilty feeling. Did I say something wrong? Everything was going good until he went to take a pee. Why the sudden change once he got back? Leaving must have given him time to dwell on his past. It was obvious that the conversation was over because he was just too far over the edge to continue. I concluded that most of his answers were somewhat normal, except for the part where he said, "… Maria ----- used to wipe my butt." I remembered hearing somewhere that a lot of psychotics fantasize about famous people.

Manhole Cover-up

After getting back to Michigan, I noticed that the weather was starting to warm up. In fact, the difference between Miami and Detroit was only a few degrees.

The weekend came and I was once again driving through the downtown Detroit area. It was Sunday at around 1:00 p.m. when I looked at the outside temperature reading from within my car. To my surprise, it read 63°F. This was quite warm for mid-February. Making my way along the riverfront, I observed that there were lots of well-dressed people walking around, taking in the sun. It looked like many of them had attended church that morning. I thought, "Where are all the homeless?" Although it seemed like a nice day to panhandle, I couldn't find anyone to interview.

Just about ready to give up, I took a ride near the ball park. It wasn't baseball season yet, so the streets were mostly vacant. Then suddenly out of the corner of my eye something looked odd as I passed a side street. So I made a quick U-turn and drove back to investigate. There I found two homeless men who were literally sleeping in the street. There was an empty parking lot nearby, so I pulled in and parked.

Walking up to them, I noticed that one man was African American and the other was Caucasian. Each had a blanket covering them and they were using the cement curb as a pillow. Steam rose up from a nearby oily manhole cover which kept them warm. The black man had very bad facial skin including visible open sores. His blanket was pulled down exposing an old soiled coat. From what I could see, it appeared to be plenty warm, but the zipper looked like it was broken. His legs protruded out from the bottom exposing red sweat pants that were covered in feces.

The Caucasian man was snoring away and seemed very content. It was apparent that his sandy brown hair had not been washed in months. Even though his beard was long, it was somewhat trimmed. At first, I did not see the guy's pants because of the blanket. But it was pulled up just enough, exposing the stained-woolly socks that covered his feet. Surprisingly, the socks did not have any holes in them. Sitting next to the two men, on the sidewalk, was a wheelchair that looked to be somewhat new. I wondered to which guy it belonged.

Realizing that my challenge was to wake them without incident, I started to clear my throat, hoping that would work. They weren't moving a muscle, so I coughed loudly, but still nothing. Wanting to get their stories, it was time to take more drastic measures. So in a loud voice I shouted, "Hey, are you awake?" Then shouting a little louder, "Can you hear me?" but still there was nothing. Thinking that they must be very tired or drunk, I bent over and placed my hand on the black man's shoulder and shook him, but once again nothing happened. Under my breath I whispered, "What the heck, he must be dead." At that instant, the black man grumbled, "What do you want?" After introducing myself, I started telling him about my endeavor, and asked if he and his friend would be willing to tell me their stories. The black man rolled over to one side and shook his friend. Believe it or not, the other man woke up with a smile on his face. He explained to his buddy why I was there and together they decided that their stories must be told.

When I revealed how much they would both be paid, the white man insisted that the money go to someone needier. I told him that upon receiving the money; it would be up to the both of them to decide what to do with it. Seeing that this was going to be a challenge I asked, "Which one of you would like to start?" Not only did they both want to talk at the same time, but their speech was so slurred and mumbled, it was almost impossible to understand. It's a good thing that I had my recorder with me.

Since I'm not using names and both may be answering the same question at the same time, (B) represents the African American gentleman and (D) is used for the Caucasian man. As always, I conveyed the rules and emphasized that there was no reason to lie. Their privacy was intact. Both assured me that they wouldn't hold back.

How old are the both of you?
(D) I'm 38. Actually, I'm an old 38. (B) I'm 40.

How long have you two been homeless?
(D) This time I've been homeless for about a year. (B) I've been on the streets for seven or eight years. I have known this guy for two years. (He must have known D before he was homeless.) He's my dog. If anything goes down, I have his goddamn back. Woops, I didn't mean to swear.

It's okay to swear. I want you to tell it like it is. Do you feel better when you swear?
(B) You're fucking right I do. (D) That's my nigga. He takes care of me.

Where are your parents?
(D) My mother just passed away, God rest her soul. My father, I never knew. I really don't want to know him.

Did your mother live a good life?
(D) My mother had her ass beat by my stepfather. That is, until I was old enough. Once I could handle myself, that never happened again. It got to the point where I could bust his ass big. (B) Look man, my daddy's been dead since I was 12 years old. I didn't even go to the funeral because he didn't do shit for me. I'm a survivor. This nigga is a survivor. I left home right after 10th grade and I have been on my own ever since. (D) I also made it to 10th grade. (B) We are survivors.

Do either of you have an addiction?
(B) We're both alcoholics. Sometimes I get the crazy shakes. We drink vodka. We don't smoke dope or do any type of drugs. But when you think about it, everything's a mother fucking drug. Drinking is a drug; eating is a drug; surviving is a drug, and living on the streets is a drug.

Damn! I just burned my ankle from the steam coming up through the manhole cover. Don't you have to be careful with that?
(B) Look at my man. He just got out of the hospital last night. See all those burns on his arms? He fell asleep on the manhole cover while drunk. (D) I woke up in a lot of pain. I asked my nigga to take me to the hospital. Look at my finger and my nose.

Did you burn them too?
(D) No, that's from frost bite. It got down to 10°F below zero last week.
(B) Put that shit in your book.

How much do you drink a day?
(B) Whatever we got, we drink it. Out here we get plenty of food. Sometimes the people from the church will give us beer. They won't give us any hard liquor, but they do know to give us some kind of alcohol, so we don't get sick. We have a lot of regulars who drive by and watch our backs. God bless them all. (D) Hey, if you ever need a white guy with brown nappy hair to work for you, I'm the one. (B) See that man who just drove by? He gave us food. They all watch out for us. Just like my home boy here. If he has to take a shit, I just throw him up in his chair and roll him to the back alley. See what I fuckin mean, we all have each other's mother fuckin back. (Now I realized who needed the wheel chair.)

Why can't you walk?
D) They told me I have cerebral atrophy$_8$ from drinking.

I see your face is all messed up. Is that from the weather?
(B) No man, I have eczema. I went to the hospital and they gave me a tube of medicine which only lasted three or four days. Hey man, see that car that just drove by. He's looking at me like if he wants to say, "Hey nigga, what's you doin?"

Do the cops ever give you a hard time?
(D) Yeah. Just last night my man went to the store to get us some liquor. A cop stopped and told me I couldn't lie in the street. I said to him, "Hey man, I can't move my legs. Why don't you just pick me up and put me in my chair." They just drove off.

Have either of you had girlfriends or been married?
(B) I have mother fuckin three kids. I love them to death. My kids are with their mama. She won't let me back because I drink too much. I don't have to be homeless you know. My sister would take me in. I choose to be homeless.

What would happen if your friend left for good and you had no one to take care of you?
(D) I would be fucked. (B) I want to be here, so I can take care of my man. I love him. His sister just stopped by with some food and blankets. (D) She won't take me in because of my drinking. In the past she set me up in a motel, but after a while it just didn't seem to work.

I remember a few years back, I read in the paper about a homeless man in this area that was killed while sitting in his wheel chair. A car drove by and ran him over. Do you know if it was done on purpose?
(B) Man, they ran that nigga right over. I believe it was a car with a bunch of white women. They were drunk, but it was an accident. He had a green cup just like me. Hey man, a while back in the summer there was this car that drove by and ran over one of my legs. I was drunk and didn't do much about it. A few days later it was starting to hurt real bad.

I pulled up my pant leg and said, "What the fuck is that!" There was this huge sore near my ankle full of maggots. I went to the hospital and the doctor told me that those maggots saved my life. The injury was all the way to my bone and I had to have surgery. It's a good thing the maggots ate out all that bad shit. I'm sure at the least I would have lost my leg. Let me stand up. Do you notice that I walk funny? It's not because I'm drunk. It's because of my injury. My balance is fucked up. People love us out here. Look, we just got these two brand new hoodies. See what the shit I'm saying man. There's love on the streets. People know we're alcoholics out here, and they still love us. (It's great to know people do care.)

I just noticed that last person a minute ago gave you a bag of food with a note in it. I then saw you whisper something in his ear. Can you tell me what the note said? And what did you say to him?
(D) The note was a prayer. I then asked him if he would lie down next to me, so we could pray together. He said no thank you because I guess he felt a little funny about that. (B) You see man, pure love. They know what we need.

I'm going to ask you guys a tough question. Do you feel God has forgotten about you?
(B) God didn't let us down, we let God down. (D) Yeah, but look how ugly God made you. (B) This guy's ugly too. (D) All kidding aside, before you go, I'm going to pray for you and that your book is successful. (I can see that these guys can joke one minute and be serious the next.)

Have either of you been in prison?
(B) Hell yeah man. I went to prison because I was carrying a thumper. You know a gun that shoots a grenade. I had it for protection, but got caught. I did time in "Jack Town." You know, Jackson Prison. It's rough in prison. You got to protect yourself or a nigga is going to come

and get your ass. The good thing is, a lot of boys I went to school with were there too. We stayed together in a group. I was 18 and skinny. I was scared as hell. I've been through some rough shit. (D) I just lay here and listen to his stories. Damn he has some crazy stories, but you want to hear this? What I'm about to tell you, I've never told anyone before. I was repeatedly raped as a child.

Do you want to talk about it?
(D) You wanted my story didn't you? I'll tell you about it. I was 12 years old living at home with my mother and stepfather. There was this guy. He was kind of a friend of my mom and dad's. This guy came into my bedroom one night. He had me do a lot of different things. One day I finally got up enough nerve and told my parents. He eventually disappeared.

What do you mean? He left and you couldn't find him anymore?
(D) No, let's just say he disappeared. You don't fuck with my family. He's gone forever. At that point I knew my family had my back. They sent me to a therapist after that. The therapist asked me what happened to the man. I just said, I don't know. (B) Well, let me tell you what happened to me. I come home one day at seven in the morning and caught my babies' mama fucking another nigga. I cracked him with a baseball bat in the head. I loved her so much, I loved her to death. But when I came home and caught them butt naked, not only did I beat him, but I beat her legs down. My kids will never know that story. They were young then, but now that they're grown they will still never know. She has her niggas' now and I don't care. She does her thing and I do mine. (D) Hey, I got a joke for you, "Why did the condom go flying across the room? Because it got pissed off." One thing you can say in your book, "I met up with these homeless mother fuckers. They're a bunch of clowns." Hey, we don't have nothing, so we might as well have a good time. You know what I admire about you? You sit with us

and care enough to hear our story. We're just like anyone else, but just got a bad break.

I offered the both of you money for your story, yet neither of you wanted it. I'm still going to give it to you, but why did you guys refuse it?
(D) What do we need the money for? People stop by all the time and give us all the food we need. We can't possibly eat it all. We collect more than enough money every day to buy our booze. Anything extra is a waste. If we do get more food or money than we need, it's handed out to our other homeless friends on the street. We try to take care of each other. (How nice is that?)

I see there is a church right behind you. Do you ever attend?
(D) We go to church every Sunday. (B) Hell, they want us to get off the streets and stay under their roof, but we would rather live out in the open. (D) I love the Lord. (B) You know why I'm not afraid to die? It is because we're dying every day on the streets. At night we have rats crawling across our bodies. That doesn't bother me, that's just the way it is. They don't bite us because we sleep on the cement. They do bite the niggas who sleep on the grass. That's where most of the rats hang out.

Would either of you consider yourself prejudice?
B) Hell no. There's niggas; there's honkies; there's spicks, I love them all. What color's your blood? I would bet it's the same color as mine, red. A nigga bleeds the same as a white man. We're all the same.

Don't you freeze some nights when it gets cold?
(B) Hell no, we always lie over this manhole cover. Sometimes it gets so hot; you sweat your balls off. (The Caucasian man needs to cover up his extremities. That must be how he ended up with frostbite on his nose and fingers.)

How much money do you collect on a good day?
D) On a good day we get $50 to $60. On a bad day we just get enough to buy a bottle. But like I say, that's all we need. Everything else is just extra. My guy here knows how to talk to the people driving by. He always says hello or he says he loves them. They know he really means it.

Do you ever hold signs? And if so, what do they say?
(B) Hell yes we hold signs. Mine usually says, "Homeless - Anything Helps." We will work too.

Will you really work?
(B) Hell yeah, I'll work.

But what about your friend. He can't work, can he?
(B) No. He can't work, but I'll work for him. He's my brother. Look, I love what you're doing. How you're telling the story of me and my brother. God bless you.

This guy who just pulled up wants to pray for you. Is that okay?
(B) Yeah, I'm ready.

(This stranger put his hand on (B's) head and prayed.)

"Father I just ask right now in the name of Jesus, that you heal this man. In the name of Jesus, open this man's eyes. In your divine grace, I command his eyes to release in the name of our lord. By the blood of the land, no more torment in the name of the lord. May you help my brothers prosper? May you raise them up to be in good health and to be above and beyond what they ever dreamt to be. Remove them from the pit of despair and into the full matrimony of the king. Father, we thank you for your love. We thank you for your provision. We thank you God; that you will never leave us or forsake us. But in the name of Jesus, I command that they be healed. Amen and Amen. I love you brothers."

(D) I love this man. God bless. (B) I love these people. They bleed like me.

I've been out here almost an hour. How come I haven't seen other homeless people?
(D) They're all over the place. I think a lot of them see you talking to us and wonder what's going on. They don't know that you're doing us a favor by telling our story. (B) See, most people don't know about us. They want to judge before knowing our story. Let them try to stay out in the mother fucking winter. Then let them judge. (D) If I can ever collect Social Security, I'm taking my friends with me. I'll spread it out the best I can. If I'm going to have money, my friends are going to have it too. (B) There's a lot of young homeless girls out here you know, and they don't have to trick either. They're taken care of. The niggas out here are going to take care of them anyway. Do you know what I'm saying? Since you've been here, look at all the food that's been dropped off. There's no way we can eat all this. You must be good luck. I guess well-to-do people aren't as intimidated when they see a clean cut person like you standing around.

Getting back to your drinking, how much did you guys drink last night?
(D) We drank about six fifths.

How can that be?
(B) That's because three of our buddies helped us.

Do you think you'll ever get off the streets?
(D) No, I think I'll die here. (B) I'm not afraid to die. When your heart stops, that's the end. I'm out here because I respect my family, my mother, brother, and sisters; they all don't want me around because I drink. I'm 40 years old. I can do what I want. Most of the time the police leave us alone. All they do is wave.

I'm going to leave now. Is there anything else you would like to say before I go?
(D) I just want to thank you one more time and God bless you. (B) Anytime you want to come back and talk, you're welcome.

As I drove off, there was a distinct realization that the more I learned about the street people, the more it affected me. Addiction is a disease and most of the time without direction or assistance it can't be turned around. On the other hand, there are many homeless people who don't want to be helped, but at least there are ways to make them feel more comfortable.

Monday came and I went shopping at Target to pick up a few things. I first purchased two large pillows. On one side they were warm and fuzzy and on the other side they were cool and smooth. Next, I bought some deodorant and a type of shampoo that didn't require water. The last thing was some over the counter eye drops. My plan was to go back the following weekend and help those guys out.

Driving home from the store, I heard on the car radio that the weather was going take a drastic change for the worse and we were going to get 10 inches of snow that night. What if those two guys were sleeping in the street and got covered with snow? A plow might come by and never see them.

The week quickly went by and when Saturday arrived I headed back to the downtown area looking for the two homeless men. The sun was shining and the temperature was in the low 40s. I arrived at the corner where we originally met, but they were not there. I must have driven up and down the streets two hours searching for them, but still no luck. I finally gave up.

I looked for them off and on another four weeks, but they were nowhere to be found. Eventually, I called a nearby church and talked to the pastor. He told me that he had not seen (B), but (D) was picked up by people from the state because of his steam burns and was taken to a nursing home for rehabilitation. I got the name of the home from the pastor and looked it up on the Internet. Many nursing homes don't have a great reputation and sure enough this one was rated only one star. I could only imagine what it must be like. The following weekend I gave (D) a visit. The home was located in a rundown area of East Detroit and the nursing home was no better. When I walked in, a man met me at the front door. He had me sign a piece of paper and then took me to the (D)'s room.

The first man I saw, after walking into the room, had a long beard and was hooked up to oxygen. Even though I remembered that (D) had a beard, there was no way that this could be him. I then peeked around a pale-blue drape that looked to be covered in blood and urine. There sitting up in the bed was (D). He looked quite different from when I saw him last. His hair was about one inch long and his beard was trimmed and groomed. He looked at me with a big smile on his face and said, "Hi Terry, how have you been?" Out of curiosity I asked, "How did you remember my name? When we met six weeks ago you were hammered." He then said with a chuckle, "The pastor called me and said you may show up. Most of what I remember from our first meeting is a blur, but I do remember your name." Then (D) offered me a seat on his wheelchair, since the small room did not have chairs for visitors.

I sat down and started looking around the room. After noticing how soiled his bed covers were I asked, "How often do they change the bedding?" He replied, "At least once a week whether it needs it or not." I was glad to see that he still had his humor. Since it was a long drive from my house to the nursing home, I had to use the bathroom. So, I asked (D) if I could use his. With a disgusted look on his face, he said,

"Okay, but don't bother to wash your hands. The sink doesn't work." I walked into the bathroom and observed that it was connecting two rooms. This meant that the bathroom was potentially shared by four people, leaving them without any running water. I left the door slightly open because the lights didn't work. The toilet seat was broken, and covered with feces and pubic hairs. Best guess, it probably hadn't been cleaned in over two weeks.

After leaving the bathroom, I went back and sat next to (D), and we continued our conversation. As we were talking, (D) grabbed a can of air freshener, pulled back the drape, and sprayed it on the patient that was in the bed next to him. He apologized for the smell and explained that it doesn't get any better. He said, "At least when I lived out on the streets there was fresh air." I asked him about the food and what was for dinner that night. With a frown on his face, he uttered, "Tonight I will get a hot dog. One thing I will guarantee, you won't gain weight around here."

I then asked if they had detoxed him from alcohol. He told me that right away they started him on morphine and Norco.[9] "But guess what? Now I'm addicted to those drugs." He continued by saying that they try to keep you sedated as long as possible. That way they can keep all the beds full. Then he began to explain about his dilemma. "Here is where the problem comes in. Not only have they got me hooked on drugs, but when it's time to leave there will be no warning. Once the money runs out from the state, they will throw me to the curb with just the clothes on my back and my wheelchair. At that point, the only thing I can do is go back to my old friends on the street and start drinking again. The only way to come down from the drugs is to drink. Just like, the only way to come down from drinking is the drugs. One thing I do know, it is one vicious cycle." I asked him if he had applied for Section 8 housing.[10] He told me that a non-profit organization affiliated with the church helped him apply several weeks ago. But if an apartment doesn't come along by the time he leaves, then nothing will change. (D) also told me he received a phone from the government, so we decided to exchange numbers. After returning home that night, I went straight upstairs and took a shower.

The next morning I called the health department and blew the whistle on the nursing home. A couple weeks later, I returned to find the water running and the food menu changed. Also, (D) was happy to report that he was approved for Section 8 housing and it was just a matter of time before he would have his own apartment. Sadly, a total of 12 weeks had passed and he was still waiting.

The Girl Next Door

It was now the middle of March and a friend told me about a young girl who was panhandling underneath a bridge at a busy intersection near where I grew up. He mentioned seeing her every morning while driving to work, so the next day I headed out. Sure enough, as I approached the bridge, there stood a young girl just as my friend had mentioned. She had on a backpack and was leaning against a large cement pillar.

I pulled the car up and introduced myself. Her round face was soft-looking, pale, and was covered with freckles. This girl just seemed too young to be on the streets. Dying to know her story, I asked for an interview. The girl replied by telling me that she was afraid and wasn't sure if I could be trusted. Not wanting to push it, I thanked her for listening, said goodbye, and drove off.

Four weeks passed and I returned to the bridge without any expectations, but to my surprise she was still there panhandling. After parking my car at the gas station across the street, I started walking towards her. She heard me approaching and turned in my direction. She was wearing the same clothes as the last time I saw her, including a red-hooded jacket with a broken zipper. Upon further inspection, I saw that her jacket was held together with safety pins that stretched from top to bottom. I asked if she remembered me from a month ago. With a half-cocked smile she said, "Yes Terry, I remember you." I thought, "How impressive is that? She remembered my name." Still wanting to get an interview, I explained that there was nothing to be afraid of and we did not have to leave her spot. The interview could be conducted right under the bridge where we were standing. She agreed and asked me how long it would take. I told her as long as she wanted it to. I could tell this was not going to be easy because not only was she apprehensive, but there was this shyness about her that reminded me of a little child.

May I ask how old you are?
I'm 26.

How far did you get in school?
I graduated from high school. My school is only a few miles from here.

Where did you grow up?
I grew up about four miles from where we stand.

Were you raised in any religion?
There was no religion in our family.

Do you believe in God?
No, not at all. I believe it's a fairy tale just like Santa Claus. (I wonder who convinced her it was a fairy tale.)

Are your mother and father still married?
They were never married. My real dad passed when I was six.

At that point, was it just your mother who raised you?
Not exactly. She got back together with her husband and they now live together. (The mother must have been married before the girls real dad came along)

Did you ever have a job?
I once had a job as a waitress and I worked at McDonalds for a little while, but flipping hamburgers didn't last long. Once I got used to the waitressing job, it lasted quite a long time.

How long did you live at home?
Till I was 16. I just wanted to get out on my own. My mother and I are still friends and we talk to each other till this day.

What made you decide to panhandle on the streets?
With no money and no job, I didn't know what to do. Everything's day by day.

Where were you living before you started to panhandle?
I was living with my sister and her dad. Then one day they just kicked me out.

Why did they kick you out?
Drug use.

What type of drugs?
Heroin.

Are you still on heroin?
Yes.

Have you gone anywhere to get help?
Yeah, but it just didn't work for me.

How did you get involved with heroin?
I was in a relationship with someone. I didn't know for a long time that she was using it, but when I found out; I got curious; I tried it.

When you tried it for the first time, how did you take it?
I used a needle. I was scared to death, but curiosity killed the cat. Now it's killing me. (She looked so innocent.)

How long did it take you to get hooked?
It doesn't take long, just a couple days. You know you're hooked when you wake up and start shaking. You almost feel like you have the flu, so you shoot up to feel better. At first, I really didn't understand. You think it's no big deal, but then it started getting serious.

How many years have you been on heroin?
On and off for about six years.

Do you do any other drugs?
I drink but don't consider myself an alcoholic. Every so often I also smoke a little marijuana.

What's the longest you've been off of heroin?
Two years.

How did you manage that?
I was in prison for two years.

What did you go to prison for?
I got in a drunk driving accident.

Is it hard to get heroin in prison?
It's accessible. The problem is that you can buy a pack of heroin on the streets for $10, but in prison its $100. So, I only did it twice. I couldn't afford it. Years ago that drug was expensive, but now it's really cheap. That's why so many people get addicted.

Do people ever stop and ask you for sexual favors?
Yeah, every once in a while they ask that, but that's one thing I won't do. I just need enough money to get by.

On the average, how much money do you collect a day.
Somewhere between $40 to $60.

How much does it cost you to live?
I do heroin three times a day. That's $30. I sleep in a nasty hotel down the street. That's $150 a week and I need a little money for food, cigarettes, and clothes.

So when you add that up, it doesn't leave you much money, does it?
Not really. Sometimes by the end of the week, I have nothing. I just live day by day.

Do the cops ever bother you?
At first they did. They would check out my ID to make sure I didn't have any warrants. Now that they know that my name is good, they just leave me alone. Every once in a while they'll come and search me, but it's just a precaution.

Since you grew up in this area, do you ever have people stop by that you know?
Every once in a while I see someone. They ask me what's wrong and I just tell them I need money. It's pretty embarrassing. This addiction is a hard thing to live with. It's real. It's a disease. I don't know which one has the worst withdraws, alcohol or heroin?

Can't you find help and kick this drug? What about your mother?
Heroin is a vicious circle. I just don't understand it. My mother will help me if I get off the drugs, but she won't help me while I'm on them. If I call her and asked for a ride somewhere, she would help me that way.

Then why don't you ask her for a ride to rehab?
I don't know. I'm confused. I'm tired of this whole situation.

You need help. How about if I call your mother and talk to her myself?
No, she won't help as long as I'm on drugs.

If you were my daughter, I would do whatever I could to get you off the streets. Don't you think your mother would do the same?
(No answer, just a sad expression)

Do you have any diseases like Hep C ?
No, the only thing I have is Lupus.

Do you take medication for that?
No.

If you don't collect enough money for the hotel, then what do you do?
Believe it or not, I always make sure to have enough money for the hotel, and then the drugs come second.

At times I have seen other people working on the exact corner that you do. Are they pretty much in the same position?
I have no idea. I just keep to myself.

Do you have any close friends?
No, it's just me.

Do you have a fear of getting better?
I have no idea. Like I said before, I don't understand life and I don't understand this drug.

Where do you get your needles?
I just get them at the store. Some places you need a prescription and other places just sell them to you.

Where do you get your drugs?
At the hotel I stay.

When you do heroin, how does it affect you?
When I'm not on it, I feel sick. When I'm on it, I feel normal. It's like taking medicine.

Earlier you said your first relationship was with a girl. Do you only date girls?
No, I would date boys or girls.

Do you have anyone who loves you now?
No!

Does your mother love you?
I'm sure she does.

Won't she do anything to help you get off the streets?
No!

Do you ever have fun?
No, every day is the same. Collect money and take drugs. I can't get out of that circle. I don't understand. I want to get better, but I can't. Nothing makes sense. I'm really scared. It's hard to explain and it's hard to understand. Either something good is going to happen or something bad is going to happen. I'll probably be doing this the rest of my life.

When I saw you a month ago, you had the same clothes on. Do you have other clothes?
A little bit. As you see, my zipper is broken on this jacket. I do have other jackets, but this one is kind of sentimental to me. I got it from an old friend.

When people stop at the light, do they ever say anything nasty to you?

Every once in a while someone may say, "Go get a job." But most people are nice. There was this one lady - every time she stopped, she would give me candy. Then after she gave me candy, she would yell at me. She would say things like, "You're pathetic out here." Finally, after the fourth or fifth time I told her to keep the candy. I feel bad enough without someone always yelling at me.

When you lay in bed at night and your mind starts to wonder, what do you think about?

I'm not really sure. But, one thing that does come to mind is, "How did I ever end up like this?" I do want to get off the streets, but this drug doesn't allow me to think that way. It's just a hard thing to explain. Getting back to my mother, she says I can't come back until I get off the drugs. It's not like turning off a light switch. Why can't she understand that?

The girl told me that time was up and she wanted to go. Figuring that she wanted to leave with the $100 to do some drugs, I agreed not to ask any more questions. As I was thanking her for the interview, she gave me a big hug not wanting to let go. Maybe for those few seconds she felt secure.

After getting back to the car, I realized that it's hard to help people in that situation. Maybe a few can be saved, but in most cases they just need to help themselves or die.

The following Friday I happened to be driving by the same intersection where I first encountered "The girl next door." It was about 4:00 p.m. and traffic was starting to get heavy. I turned the corner and there she was, wearing the same tattered clothes, holding a crumpled sign. After pulling into a gas station across the street, I watched her for a while and could see that she wasn't collecting much money. So, I got out of the car and crossed the street to check on how she was doing. I asked how she felt and if anything had changed. She explained that everything was the same, but then started to tell me about the hotel.

While shaking her head back and forth she told me that the hotel should be closed. Then with a disgusted look she said, "The only people that stay there are drug dealers, drug users, and prostitutes. My room is full of bed bugs and roaches. The hotel is also covered in rats. It's such a nasty place to stay." I asked, "Are you ready to leave?" With no hesitation she replied, "I guess I'm just not ready." I got a little frustrated and put my hands on her shoulders. Then I shook her as if to say, "Wake up and get your shit together." She immediately cringed with pain and explained that her veins were all dried up and that she had to shoot directly into her muscles. The girl then pulled up her sleeve revealing a large open sore. After I apologized, she told me it didn't matter because there was no way I could have known.

I had to wonder how controlling this drug really was. Here's a young girl with a whole life ahead of her and she would rather live with drugs and bugs than straighten herself out. I gave her my phone number and said that if she needed anything to give me a call. Like many homeless people, she had a phone that was supplied by the government.

Homeless Depot

"What shocks me is that so many people leave care and become homeless, and when you're homeless you get into crime, prostitution and drugs, and it is a vicious circle. That's what we need to change."
Samantha Morton [actress]

It was now the middle of April and the week seemed to be dragging on, but Saturday finally arrived. The morning started out gloomy with the temperature at around 40°F.

I left my home at 11:00 a.m. and headed back to the downtown area near where I previously had success finding people to interview. I drove down to within a few blocks of the ball park and noticed an African American man reaching into a garbage can. Pulling up beside him, I lowered the window and asked if he could help me. He was very polite and asked what he could do. Not wanting to make any assumptions, I asked if there were any homeless people in the area that could be interviewed for my project. Surprised at my inquiry he replied, "You see, there's a place three blocks away where most of the homeless in this area hang out." "How many people live there?" I questioned. He cracked a smile and said, "Around 6,000." I thought to myself, "Oh my God! There's a whole subculture that lives right around the corner and I didn't even know it." I asked, "Would you be willing to show me where the place is." He replied, "Sure, it won't be a problem."

Expressing my involvement with the homeless, I inquired as to whether he would be interested in telling me his life story. The man agreed, so I invited him to get into my car where it was warm. He had a very strong odor that I didn't want to linger, so I grabbed a blanket from the back and draped it over the front seat. Not wanting to hurt his feelings, I told him that the blanket was to help him keep warm. He got in the car and with the heat turned up, we started our conversation.

Can you tell me your age?
I'm 53 years old sir.

What is your nationality?
I'm African American and my grandmother was American Indian. She had papers to prove it.

Did you grow up with your mother and father?
Yes, they're just 20 years older than I am. They're both 73 now. We've lived in Detroit for 52 years.

Are they still together? The reason I ask is because many homeless people come from broken families.
They're still together even though my father hardly ever sticks around the house.

How far did you go in school?
I went to college. In fact, I had quite a bit of college. I went to four colleges. I went to Henry Ford Community, Wayne County Community College, Eastern University, and Southern University.

I don't want this to sound wrong, but why don't you speak with a street lingo?
This is just the way I am. I'm not trying to impress anyone, but I like to talk whatever the situation requires. I just want to be like everyone else that I'm hanging with at the time.

Have you ever been married or had a girl friend?
In high school I was very popular. I was the type of guy that girls liked to hang out with. I was quarterback on the football team and I was very good. We won a state championship. I played other positions, but my main position was quarterback. Even though my mother and father

stayed together all those years, if you heard about my dysfunctional family, you would have to wonder how in the heck I did so well in school.

We'll get into that, but first tell me if you had any religious upbringing?
At first, we lived in the same house with my grandparents. We were Baptist. They made sure to take their children and grandchildren to church every Sunday. We all moved up to Detroit from Louisiana when I was 14 months old. My mother and father finally decided to get married five years after I was born.

Do you have any brothers and sisters?
I have three sisters and one brother.

Are any of them homeless?
No, but my brother, he's 14 years younger than I am. He's 39. I guess he wouldn't mind me telling you about the way he lives. My brother is involved in a life of crime. He has been a Detroiter all his life. He's been in prison 15 out of the last 19 years. Growing up, he would mimic anyone who was in a gang. His first time in prison was at age 19.

What did he go to prison for?
He ended up with 18 counts of armed robbery. He was also involved in selling drugs. Three of his friends were murdered. Once that happened, he decided to take it out on society.

Is he still in Jail?
No.

Now that he's out of jail, is he reformed?
He can't stop. His involvement in crime won't allow it. He walks the streets freely, but crime has him by the throat.

Let's get back to your upbringing. You said that I wouldn't believe how well you did in school because of your dysfunctional family. Will you tell me about it?

My mother started to sell heroin at age 26. My father also sold it and was hooked since he was 18. If a purchase was more than he could use, it would be sold off. Just like my brother, my father is also a criminal, but much smaller. Any building that has low security, my father will break into. My dad is unemployable. By the time he was 28 years old, he had five convictions and did time in Jackson Prison. My father is part of a family that had a total of 24 boys and girls. With his personality, he gets along with everyone. My dad doesn't carry a gun or knife, but again, he just gets along with everyone. (Even though his situation wasn't created by a broken family, I now understood why this guy was on the streets.)

Does your father still take drugs?

He's still on heroin. It's been 55 years for him. From the very beginning he would physically abuse my mother. He would beat her the same way he would beat his children. It was all because of frustration. When my younger sister was born, my father brought her home from the hospital while my mother was still admitted. When he walked into the house for the first time holding my sister, he asked me if I knew how to warm up a baby bottle. I told him yes and I was only five at the time. He handed her over to me and left. That's the way he was, always in and out. The house was just a stopping place. He never stayed around to raise us. He liked to party too much. His dependency on drugs had become a burden in regards to his family. At five years old I was able to fix bottles with formula and I was even able to change diapers. I got pretty good at it. I watched my mother do it and just picked it up that way. Just so you know, my mother never took drugs, only sold them. She took a pill every now and then, but not enough to get hooked.

How did your father make most of his money?

He had many friends. If he didn't steal or get it from my mother, his friends would take care of him. He has quite a personality. Heroin wasn't a nasty habit for him. What I mean by that is there was never any blood running down his arm. He hid it very well. My dad never got sick or had Hep C. Even though he had a lot of problems, you could never tell it. His family was so large, he just blended in. They would always watch his back.

Growing up, did you get involved in drugs or crime?

No, not at all. I did do a little marijuana, but that's it. There were a lot of criminals on my father's side. My father's family, that lived in Louisiana, they would hop on moving trains and steal everything on board. But they were really nice people. They are close and have very strong family values. They have a community of their own within the neighborhood. The family's not ignorant or foolish, and they're good looking people too.

Right after high school, did you go straight to college?

Yes, I wanted to play football. I decided to stick with Eastern because it's where a lot of African American football players had a better chance to get into the big times. If you pick a school that is a Mid-American conference, your chances go way up. You don't want to get with the University of Michigan or State. There's too much competition. They have athletes from all around the world. At Eastern, I played through winter drills and I went all the way through the spring game. I was just a part of the team like everyone else.

How did you pay for college?

I applied for financial aid and I also got a loan. Eastern Michigan lasted three semesters and then I went to Wayne County Community college downtown. From there I moved to Louisiana to pursue a football carrier. There was a coach down there with the most wins in the history of NCAA division one. His name was Eddy Robinson.[11] He produced so many NFL professional football players. Arriving in Louisiana, I wanted to go to Grambling University, but instead ended up at Southern. That college was right in my grandmother's home town. That gave me a place to stay. I went down there and got into camp. Finally, I got my opportunity. I was a defensive back. I went two weeks where there wasn't one pass reception that was completed on me. That was until the NFL scouts showed up and I started feeling the pressure. To me, it was an amazing effort.

So, why didn't you make it?
Well, the Washington Red Skins had a player. You may remember him. His name was Darrell Green.[12] He was 40 years old. That was the very position I was to get. I would have had to take his position. Even though he was 40 years old, he was still one of the fastest on the team. I just didn't have the experience to take his place. There is so much to know in football. You have to learn to be an athlete and know what athletes do. You need the right attitude, excitement, and aggressiveness. It's such a science. Experience wins every time.

So needless to say, you didn't make it?
Yes you're right, but let me tell you something. At nine years old I had jumped 50 inches in the high jump. And, in ninth grade the coach said I had beaten the world record in the 220 yard dash. So you see, the elders understood why it was so hard for players to catch a pass against me, but experience wins out.

After you left college, what happened then?
I began to realize that I've been profiled since I was a baby by the police.

Can you explain that a little better?

As I told you before, my whole family was involved in crime. Our name was high on the list with the Detroit police. Every time we moved, it was next door to gangs. We didn't plan it that way, it just happened. Every time we moved since the 60's, we didn't just move next to gangs, we moved next to the "leaders" of the gangs. They always seemed to live on our block. Many times they would live across the street or directly next door. The police thought we followed them on purpose, but it was just a coincidence. The police began to build a case upon that. I was putting up with this my whole life. Even when I was a little boy, the police would hassle me thinking that I was involved with crime. The police thought that they had something so good that they just weren't going to let it go. They pushed our family so hard. My father ended up jumping on me.

I don't understand, what do you mean?

Here I was going to college minding my own business and my father took advantage of the situation. He would beat me as if to show the police that he was trying to straighten me out. In reality, he was taking the pressure off of himself and putting it on me. You see, I was really trying to make something of myself. I took two IQ tests. The first one I scored 132 and the other one I scored 133. In elementary school I was the chosen one to give speeches to the student body, and as I got older, I would win all my spelling bees. I won so many that they realized that I was a gifted student. I remember they brought in a person from the University of Michigan just to give me that IQ test. I was a highly educated African American student living in the inner city. When I scored that high IQ, I was taken to the University of Michigan and met the students that were in the African American study group. This was in 1970. I was eight years old.

Getting back to what I asked you before. You never used drugs or alcohol?

In college I drank a little, and I do some pot. For a while I had a problem with rock cocaine. I can tell you some stuff about that too. I witnessed two murders. They happened in one 48 hour period. You have to realize, I've been around drugs all my life. For a friend to be over my house selling drugs was no big deal. I wasn't selling them, but I was the door man. I knew what was going on. And besides, I had a good personality. That's a good combination to help someone sell drugs. There was so much jealousy on the street. The other dealers thought that the guys in my house were taking away their business. When the buyers came to the front door, I was the one to meet them. They were very comfortable around me. There was no presence of fear when I answered the door.

We started selling at the beginning of the weekend and by the second day, people got killed. I don't blame the guy. He had to protect himself when his life was threatened. Here's how it happened. This guy came in and pulled a gun. He said to give him all the drugs. One of my guys pulled his gun and started shooting. He missed and the buyer ran out the door. The two guys who were in my house went chasing after the man, but then they came upon another man who was hiding in the bushes. He had an automatic weapon and killed them both.

Why didn't they come back after you?

I guess because they knew I was only the door man and was no threat.

Did the police ever get involved?

You see, with those high powered weapons, they're able to fend the police off. These drug people, they rob businesses and all the police do is watch them. The police will shoot from a distance, but they're afraid.

I understand that all this happened over 30 years ago, but what did you do after college?

I went back to live at home. When I told you before that my father beat me, my parents ended up putting me in a psych ward. At that time my dad hit me several times on the head with a heavy blunt object. When the police showed up they said, "You're going to have to leave the house." My father made me look like the bad guy. I was 20 years old. The police didn't arrest me. They just dragged me off to a psych ward.

What was the diagnosis?

Paranoid schizophrenic.[13]

Did you think the diagnosis was correct?

Not in the beginning. I didn't think there was a problem at all, but then as time went on you think, "You know, there could be something to this." This was back during the days before they shut all the wards down. There were people in the wards with insurance and they were just trying to get some rest. The psych wards were all over the city of Detroit. At one time or another, I must have been in all of them. (At this point of our conversation he still seemed somewhat normal.)

What was it like in the wards?

It wasn't bad there. If you didn't have insurance, they would kick you out after two months. They always had things for you to do. There were many different activities. You would have plenty of food. If you didn't have money, they would give you indigent money. With that you could buy all the cigarettes, candy, and pop you wanted. It was very involved, but it did eat up all the taxpayers' money. I was interviewed one time by the local paper. I told them that living in a psych ward was like living as a very wealthy person. You were treated as if you were at a hospital estate. Sometimes I would walk out one of the exits and find beautiful picnic grounds that were fenced in. I was amazed with the beautiful tables, the nice green grass, and the wonderful trees.

At that point, did you have a job?
Because of the psych wards, I was pretty much unemployable. But for a while I did work on someone's political campaign.

Where did you live after you got out of the psych wards?
During those days, I went to what was called, an "adult foster care home." I got along with everyone. I learned in later life that one of the criteria for going to a psych hospital was being poor. Back then if you needed work and didn't have anywhere to go, you ended up in the ward. They would even take children in. At the adult foster care home I won an award for good conduct as one of the new clients. This was when I was 22 years old. I forgot to tell you how I was abandoned three times. At nine years old my father had me go with him to the pool hall. He played one game and we left on the bus. He took me to an old cemetery and dropped me off. The police found me and took me home. I remember back at age seven my mom couldn't take care of us four kids anymore. So, she called my aunt who lived in Louisiana and surrendered us to her. We lived down there for a year before we came back. There was also the time, when I was one year old, that my father dropped me off at his baby sister's and left. It was just for a few days, but it affected me mentally. I was prepared for adulthood at age five.

Getting back to my 20s, there became a realization that I was getting caught up in the system. The city of Detroit was falling apart. I tried going around talking to people, but no one would listen. My past was full of hope and prosperity, but with Detroit falling apart, it was all coming to an end.

How many adult foster care homes did you stay in over the years?
Four all together. I remember at the first home there was this white lady who treated me very badly. She wouldn't give me breakfast or lunch. I don't want this to sound wrong, but she reminded me of you. One day I got mad at her. She got up from her chair and I pushed her down. I

didn't push her that hard, but she fell to the ground. It was like when you watch a basketball game and a player does a fake fall, so the other player would get a penalty. At this point in my life, I wouldn't do anything to hurt someone. But because of that, the owner of the home sent me back to the psych ward. I believe it was all in a plan. I had two months of SSI checks come while I was in the ward. All I ended up with was one 10th of the money which was $150. I believe the husband and wife planned it together and got the rest. These are the kind of things that happen to young black men in the inner city. Don't get me wrong. I'm not prejudice. I just got caught up in the system. So as you can see, between the police and the government, it makes it absolutely impossible for a young man like me to function.

Did you have a good relationship with any police while growing up?
Absolutely I did. A policeman found me at Southeastern High School. We became friends. He won the title of Mr. Michigan 12 times in a row. He said we were friends for life because I had a good workout ethic. He asked me all about the way I worked out, and I wrote it down for him. He used it ever since. I was 17 at the time. We're still friends to this day. Then, when I was at Eastern University there was this Washtenaw County Sheriff who became my friend. So you see, I can make friends with anyone.

There's still a big time line between your early 20s and the age you're at today. Can you fill me in?
It was then that I really realized that the police were still profiling me because of my family history. It seems they would try to take advantage of a situation just to impress women. It got to the point it was humorous.

But after all those years, why didn't they just leave you alone?

Because they thought there was enough evidence on me to take me in, but they had nothing. They could not stop because of an idea that they just couldn't let go. But then after all those years, they realized that sin would get them in trouble, and then sin would get them out of trouble. They couldn't go back and change the record because that would get them in trouble. Sin makes you understand that the Devil will win the war when it comes to good versus evil. You don't realize that the Devil is just making a fool of you. Around here the Devil is in charge instead of God because there are so many sins. God can't help you because the Devil keeps taking you down. It's the people who sin that helps build up the Devil's confidence. It's all a state of mind. (At that point I thought I was starting to lose him.)

You realize that the way you're talking right now doesn't make a lot of sense?

The police hit me. It's what they do to gang members. I'm not a gang member, but they lived all around me, so they thought I must have been one.

If a cop drove by right now and saw you sitting in my car, would they think we were doing some kind of drug deal?

I think it would frighten them to think that they might have to arrest me. They would have to profile me, come up with nothing, and throw me back in a psych ward. It's almost childish to think like the police do.

You know the Devil works on putting men down. In church the pastor says, "Men are destructive people." or they say, "Men are chaotic." Women - they hear it all the time. It makes a witch out of them. Women feel they can't trust men, so they don't want to hear what men have to say. Women think they choose their men wisely and look who they end up with. They usually shut the good people out of their lives and end up with the bad. The churches tell the women to practice witchcraft.

They're not teaching them to be a virgin mother with child. They're teaching them to hate men. If you have someone telling you over and over, "Men are bad, men are bad," they're going to start to believe it. That's not what women should be taught. If you teach them that in church, you're teaching them witchcraft. (I can see where that would make sense in his mind.)

How long have you been homeless?
Shortly after I left college. (He must have considered himself homeless when he first came home from college, while in the psych wards, and adult foster care.)

Where do you sleep at night?
Anywhere I can. I would stay in abandoned buildings, parks, and shelters.

How do you keep warm?
I would always bundle up. If I'm in a building, I try to find one without other people sleeping there.

Do you know most of the people out here?
You wouldn't believe all the friends I have. They come from all walks of life. One time I talked to a therapist that held Bible studies on the side. She shouldn't have done that, but she did. One day she asked me to come to her Lutheran church and try out for the choir. When I sang, she said I was gifted. While at that church, I picked up a Bible one day and read a passage. Then my whole life started to make sense. I couldn't put the Bible down. It made me humble, but there is so much confusion in the world. I'm driven to show people what is happening in this city with the profiling.

How do you get your food?
Soup kitchens. I also get money from bottles in trash cans.

You have a grocery cart. Where did you get it from?
I find them all over the place. When I find one, I take it back to its original store.

Did you have any women in your life when you went to school?
Sir, I was like a NFL caliber player back when I was in school. I would get as many women as I could handle. They came and they went.

Do you have any children?
I don't.

Earlier you told me all the different places you slept. Where did you sleep last night?
I slept at a friend's house.

Do you ever panhandle?
I tried it a few times, but I don't like the way women look at me. So, nowadays I pick and choose who I ask.

Since you don't do drugs or drink, what do you need money for?
I ask myself that same question sometimes. People give me five and ten dollar bills. Many times I give it to the other homeless. I give it to people, so they won't get lost in this world. They need to go out and shop or buy themselves something to eat.

Do you ever have fun?
I have fun all the time. I go to shows or concerts.

Where do you get the money for that?
I get a SSI check every month. I've been getting it since I was a young man.

How much do you get a month?
I get $715 a month.

How do you spend the money?

First of all, when I get my check, I take it to a check cashing place. I show them my ID and they cash it for a $15 fee. It's hard to mention it, but I have a female friend who has a problem with heroin. I don't like her doing that drug because it's so stressful. So, I support her habit with marijuana. When I get my SSI check, I spend it all on weed. By the time it's all gone, she kicks me out until the following month when I can buy some more.

Is she your girlfriend?

No, not really. I just stay over her house till all the marijuana is gone and then I have to leave. For the past three years I have spent every penny I get on her. (I wondered how he paid for the shows and concerts.) You see sir; women have always been a big concern in my life. The homeless women either drinks too much, they're on heroin or they're on cocaine. I try to do what I can, when I can. I help the women and not the men. If the women are in the position where they need help, they'll let the men do whatever they want to them. When the men see a woman in trouble, they know it is easy pickins.

When you give the women money are you expecting something in return?

I'm a man and things like that run across my mind. I won't take advantage of them at all, but if they want to build a relationship, that would be okay. If I do give them money and they still offer me sex, I'll turn it down. Because at that point, I would feel obligated to have a relationship. Many of the homeless men try to find a woman on public assistance. That's like an extra bonus. They want to do what a lot of the black men did in the 1970's. Have babies and leave. This is what people don't realize. Because of the Vietnam War and civil rights movements, a lot of men walked out on their women. This is why we have an overabundance of street people now. They all came from broken homes in the 70s.

Earlier you offered to show me the large group of homeless people. Would you still do that?
Sure I will.

(At that point we proceeded to drive down to the area where all the homeless hung out. As we turned around the last corner to our destination, I was totally taken by surprise. People were standing everywhere. They were lined up all along the sidewalks. Many were standing under makeshift gazebos. There were also men and women just hanging out in the middle of the street. It reminded me of people waiting for a train at a long depot.)

What do you think they're all talking about?
It's a lot of small talk, but most of them are dealing drugs. Don't come out here at night. It wouldn't be safe.

I drove the man back, paid him, and headed home.

Like Father, Like Son

It was the following Tuesday afternoon, just three days after my last interview. While driving home from work, I noticed two panhandlers working corners that were directly adjacent to each other. Having seen teams working corners before, I wondered if they knew each other. They were both Caucasian males. One looked older than the other and was rather rough looking - as if he was an old time boxer. The younger man was well dressed. I decided to ask the older man for an interview first. Driving my car into a nearby gas station, I was a little nervous about approaching him because of the way he looked. As I was crossing the road, the man looked towards me and smiled. I felt that a load had just been lifted from my shoulders. It's funny what a little smile can do for a person. After shaking hands, I explained my mission and asked if he would be willing to submit to an interview. He replied, "Sure I would and if you'd like, you can ask my son across the street as well."

I thanked him and went across the street to talk with his son. The boy wasn't nearly as friendly as his father. My gut feeling was that he thought there was something up my sleeve. I assured him that the interview would be for my book and nothing else. The son explained that he was 21 years old and had been panhandling for the past three years. His goal was to write a book about his experience on the streets. Thinking that he thought I might be stealing his idea, I told him that my book was about homeless people in general and that his book would be an autobiography. Then I said, "Just remember to keep your book interesting." With an attitude he replied, "I don't care if anyone reads it or not." After mentioning that his father consented to meet me at 6:30 p.m. the next evening, I asked him if that would be okay. He agreed and said that we would all meet at their Tahoe truck, which was parked a half mile down the road in the Panera Bread restaurant parking lot. We shook hands and said goodbye.

The next evening, I found them waiting patiently next to their black 1995 Tahoe truck. The vehicle was in bad shape, being held together by wire and tape. The inside was filled to the brim with almost anything you could imagine. I asked the father where they lived and he said, "You're looking at it. This truck and the parking lot is our home." Then stretching his arms as far apart as he could, the father yelled, "This is all mine!"

As we were walking into the restaurant, I told them that they could order anything on the menu. The father wasn't hungry and just ordered a bowl of chicken noodle soup. The boy ordered Chicken Alfredo which came with a small loaf of bread. We picked up our food and sat down at a table. The son was still carrying a very bad attitude, so I wasn't sure how far this interview would go.

I reached into my pocket, pulled out my small recorder, and set it on the table. The boy quickly responded in a loud voice, "You're not going to record us are you?" Hoping to get a laugh, I replied, "At my age the memory is the first thing that goes." I didn't get a smile from either of them and thought, "Oh, this is a great way to start." I looked over at the boy and noticed that he was picking apart the small loaf of bread. It reminded me of someone pulling feathers out of a pillow and throwing them all over the floor. This boy definitely had some issues that were sure to come out in our conversation.

For this interview the letter (F) represents the father and the letter (S) is used for his son.

I'm going to put the recorder a little closer to you (F) because you're harder to understand. Why do you talk with a slur?
(F) One time I was jumped by 10 black guys and they beat me to where I was in a coma for five months. Both my speech and balance are bad. Every time I get pulled over by a cop, they give me a breathalyzer test.

How old are the both of you?
(S) I'm 21. (F) And I'm 51.

Are either of you married?
(F) I was never married. The last time I was with my son's mother was 15 years ago. (S) I'm too young to get married.

(I then noticed that the boy was taking the torn pieces of bread and tearing them into even smaller pieces.)

Were your mother and father married?
(F) Years ago, but they got divorced when I was young.

Are they still alive?
(F) Oh yeah, they're both alive. I talk to both of them every couple weeks.

Did your parents bring you up in any religion?
F) No, nothing, but I believe in God. Life is great.

Do you believe in God too?
(S) Yes, I do.

When you panhandle, what does your sign read?
(F) "Anything Helps, God Bless."

And what does yours say?
(S) "Homeless, Please Help." (F) We're not homeless. The whole world is our home.

Did you ever have a job?
(F) After I got out of prison.

What were you in prison for?
(F) A lot of bad things. Breaking and entering, and possession of a hand gun.

Why were you stealing? Were you doing drugs?

(F) No, I was just hanging around with the wrong people.

Why did you have a gun?

(F) This one place we broke into, they had guns, so we just stole them.

Was your son alive when you were in prison?

(F) No, he wasn't born yet. After I got out of prison, I worked in die casting.

How long were you in prison?

They gave me 20 years. I was out in five years and four months. Then I did 18 months in a correction center. From there I got an apartment.

When did you meet your son's mother?

(F) Actually, I meet her while I was still in prison.

How many years ago were you in prison?

(F) It was 30 years ago. When I was in there, I did exactly what I was told.

(I kept talking to the father because the son didn't seem interested in participating.)

Do you have any brothers or sisters?

(F) I have four sisters and they're all doing well. None of them are homeless, but they hate me because I hold a sign.

Do you think you're capable of getting a job?

(F) I can work, but I don't think I'd be very good because of my handicap. My balance is off.

Do you get any assistance from the government?

(F) No, I don't. Church people drive by all the time and give us a card to their church, but they don't want to help you. They want to take you in, so they can look good. When I go there, they tell me that there's not much they can do for me, so I just go back to my corner. If you're allowed to stay at their church, you have to be in at 6:00 p.m. and out at 6:00 a.m. The way it is now, I can do what I want when I want. Life is great.

How long have you been homeless?
(F) It's been around three years, but I'm not homeless. I have my truck. Before that, I lived in an apartment.

Why are you in this town?
(F) We go all over. We even go out of state. It's not that the money slows up, we just like to travel. God loves us.

Turning towards the boy - Did you graduate from high school?
(S) I made it through 11th grade. After that I wanted to travel.

Do you have any talents?
(S) I don't know. I really don't feel comfortable talking to you. My dad has already told you his life story. Last night we decided to tell you the truth, but I didn't think my dad would tell you so much. (F) I really didn't say anything wrong.

Did you ever have a job?
(S) Yeah, working with my dad, but it fell apart.

Isn't it harder to panhandle than to work?
(F) It can be. It gets pretty boring out there. My son passes the time by listening to music when he's out on the street.

What are you working on there? It looks like quite a project tearing apart your bread.
(S) [No answer.]

How do you feel about your son panhandling?
(F) He can do whatever he wants. If he wants to get a job, that's okay too.

Where do you go when it gets real cold out?
(F) As long as I have a vehicle, we're okay. Actually, I would rather be in the cold than down South in the heat.

Have you ever had a girlfriend?
(S) Yeah, at one time. (F) It's hard for him to keep a girlfriend because we're on the move all the time.

Do you make good money?
(F) Hey, we don't do anything wrong. Everything we do is legal. If the police want to arrest me and put me in jail, that's okay. I will have a warm place to stay and three meals a day. I have no reason to lie about what I do. (S) What is the name of your book? I replied, "It's called *One Leg and a Cup*" (I felt like the son was testing me to see if I was really writing a book.)

Isn't there an ordinance in some areas against panhandling?
(F) There's no law against holding a sign. People hold signs all the time when they advertise for their stores. There are some places where they don't want you to hold a sign, but you can still ask for money. There's no law against that. (I still felt as if they both thought I was up to something.)

Do you guys ever save money?
(F) We save a little here and there.

Do you have a bank account?
(F) I've had bank accounts in other people's names.

Getting back to that book you want to write about yourself, are you a good writer?
(S) No, but I have friends who can write for me.

What states do you panhandle in?
(F) We've gone to places like Florida and Las Vegas. I love to travel.

What about a person who can't afford to travel? What should they do?
(F) Grab a sign and you can go wherever you want.

Has anyone ever done anything bad to you?
(F) Not really. I love everyone. I did have something weird happen the other day. There was this guy who stopped in the middle lane and took a picture of me. I'm not sure what that was all about. It's nobody's business what I do. I'm not hurting anyone.

Is it hard for you to panhandle?
(S) No, we just make a little money and go back to our truck.
(I believed the boy was thinking that I was trying to figure out how much money he made.)

At the beginning you told me that you were beat up. What exactly happened?
(F) I was just walking down the street and 10 niggers jumped me out of nowhere. Like I said, they hurt me pretty bad. That's why I wobble so much. One day I was just walking down the street and a cop pulled over and asked me, "How much have you had to drink?" Fuck him. He should just mind his own business.

Do either of you do drugs?
(S) I do a little marijuana. (F) I smoke it too. I have a card. (The son started to look angry.)

You don't seem too happy right now. What's wrong?
(S) My dad just can't keep his mouth shut. He wants to tell you everything. (F) I have nothing to hide.

Does it bother you that your dad just wants to talk?
(S) He can say what he wants. I'm just not going to tell you my life story. (F) Look, I want one thing and one thing only. I want to go to heaven. You know, life ain't bad. I love life.

Yesterday your dad told me you both have a phone and a laptop. Is that something homeless people usually own?
(S) No answer. (F) Just because we're homeless doesn't mean we can't own a few nice things.

What's the worst thing you've ever seen on the streets?
(S) The worst thing is the homeless bums.

What's a homeless bum?
(S) A homeless drunk. (I'm starting to understand that there is an upper, middle, and lower class with the homeless.)

Would you rather panhandle than get a job?
(S) I would much rather do this. Let me tell you why. With a job I have to be there every morning at a certain time and leave at a certain time. Then you have to wait for your money at the end of the week. With panhandling, I get money every day and make my own hours.

What's the most money you ever got from one person?
(F) One day a man gave me $500 and gave my son $500. (S) That wasn't me. (F) Oh yeah, it was my son's friend. (It sounded like the son wanted the father to change his story.)

(At that point the son got up from the table and left the restaurant.)

Do you think I'm doing this for any reason other than my book?
(F) No, I don't. But if you are, I'll kill you. Just kidding, I better watch what I say. Sometimes I worry about my son, but he's his own boss. No matter what I say, he thinks I'm always wrong.

(The son then walked back into the restaurant.)

What's wrong?
(S) My dad and I talked about this and all he wants to do is run his mouth off.

You do realize this book might help people like you?
(S) Here's what I realize. I started doing this one year before my dad got involved. He came in and joined me later. He made it into a job and now he's running his mouth off.

Do you guys split your take?
(S) I'd rather not even talk about it. (F) I don't even know what I did wrong. (S) You just told him we made $500 each. You can't keep your mouth shut. You tell the truth to everyone but me.

(The son got up and left again.)

Don't you think he has a pretty tough life?
(F) I love him, but it's his way or the highway. I'm getting tired of it. He's just going through a hard time. We're here to help each other, not hate each other. He has problems, but we all have problems.

Do you do anything for entertainment?
(F) I like watching movies. We have a DVD player in the car.

Let me ask you this. Let's say it's two in the morning and you have to go to the bathroom, where do you go?
(F) If I have to take a pee, we have bottles in the car. You just can't show your pecker. If I have to go the other way, I walk down to the gas station. Remember, I'm not homeless. I have the whole world out there.

When you're sick, where do you go?
(F) I never get sick, but I do wonder where my son went. I hope he's out by the car. I worry about him all the time. What did I do wrong? Why is he so pissed off at me?

(He then tried calling his son on the phone, but there was no answer.)

Do you have any plans for the future?
(F) I just want to go to heaven.

You're not in any hurry to die are you?
No, but if God wanted to take me right now, I would go.

Since you were not raised in a religion, when did you find God?
(F) I found him in prison.

(The father's phone rang and it was his son. The dad said, "We're done. We'll be out shortly.")

What's he worried about?
(F) He's just stupid. He doesn't know what's going on. We better go. I gave you my phone number, so call me if you need something. (I also gave him my phone number.)

We quickly finished dinner and walked outside looking for the boy. Approaching the truck, we could see him sitting in the driver's seat facing straight ahead. His father knocked on the window, but the boy just ignored him. After a second knock, the door swung open and the distinct smell of marijuana came pouring out of the cab. The boy noticed me and apologized for the way he acted. As I said goodbye and walked away, I could still hear the two of them arguing in the distance.

That night I received a call from the father at around 9:30 p.m. He started drilling me with a bunch of questions. I figured his son was the one who put him up to it. They were questions like, "How do you spell your name again?" and "What's the name of your book?" After giving him the answers, he kindly thanked me and hung up.

It's Not All Cracked Up to What It Used to Be

"Clearly, there are a thousand and one scenarios for how someone can slip through the cracks. I'll walk down the street and see a homeless person, and I'll want to stop them and say, How did this happen? Where's your mother? Are you physically ill? Mentally ill?"
William Baldwin [actor]

The following week I received a call from my friend Bob, who is a Detroit firefighter. He told me about this guy who was squatting in an old abandoned house directly behind his station. Bob and the man happened to be on a first name basis. He explained to the guy that I was writing a book about the homeless and asked if he would like to participate. The man agreed and Bob said he would call me once the fellow was ready to talk.

At 7:30 p.m. the next Saturday, I received the call from Bob. He told me the man was ready to tell his story, but the guy seemed to be a little drowsy. After getting the directions to the fire station, I headed off to meet him.

When I arrived, there was an African American man sitting on a bench directly in front of the station. Bob came out and introduced us. The man was dressed in soiled-dark clothes and had a pungent order about him. His speech was rough and his face was puffy. At first it was hard to understand him, but after a few minutes I was picking up on his dialect. Bob took both of us to a waiting room inside the station. After we sat down, I made it clear that he would receive $100 for the interview. The man immediately started shaking his hand back and forth as if to say, "What-ever." I began moving my hand back and forth in the same motion and asked, "What does this mean?" He replied with a cocky attitude, "I'm just taking your offer with a grain of salt. I've been burned so many times, I don't care if you give it to me or not." After assuring him one more time that he would receive the money, I started asking questions.

You're hard to understand, why is that?
I just woke up. I told Bob I won't be a "dick." I'll be as nice as possible. It's not normal for me to even act like a dick. That would be unusual if I did. I'm not even a drunk. This is how I sound when I just wake up. What day is it? Oh my God, it's Saturday. I just slept for 15 hours. I told Bob I would commit myself to you, so let's get on with the questions. I'll treat you properly.

How old are you?
I'm 52 as of last month.

What religion were you brought up?
I was brought up Baptist.

Do you believe in God?
Absolutely I do.

How do you feel about the way you turned out?
I feel rebellious.

Rebellious against whom?
Rebellious against myself. The only way I can get out of the drugs is to cut my ties.

Since high school, what was the longest you went without drugs?
Once I went a whole year. In 1988 I went into a program, but when I got out it started all over again. Back then I was happy with just weed and mescaline.[14]

We will get back to the drugs later. Let's talk about your family. Are your mother and father still alive?

Let me think. No, my real parents are not alive. I was adopted. My mother died in 1992. She went in for a gallbladder operation and had a stroke. They put her on life support and I had to sign the papers to let her go. My real father died when I was seven years old. He was into drugs. The police shot and killed him.

Do you have any brothers or sisters?

Yes, I do. My new parents adopted my brother and sister. My brother, who is two years younger than me, is in the Secret Service, and my sister is 10 years younger.

How far did you get in school?

I got my GED. My stepdad made sure of it.

Did you get a job after school?

Yeah, I started working in a Chatham grocery store. They're not around anymore.

When did you leave home?

My mother first kicked me out when I came home one day on LSD.[15] I humbly knocked on the front door, but I saw the reflection of my stepfather through the window. I thought it was Satan himself. From there I ran around the house to try and sneak in through the side window and ended up crushing the awning. After that, she put me in the Northville State Hospital.[16] When I got out, my mother emancipated me. She let go of all legal ties. I was 17 at the time.

Why did she let you go?

Not only because of the drugs, but also it had to do with the white people that I was hanging out with. I remember one day, I ran away from home. I snuck out by taking a penny and unscrewed the bathroom window. After I left, I was living in the back of a 7-Eleven. This friend of mine was a cashier and let me stay there.

What kind of drugs did you take?
I first started smoking marijuana out of a corn cob pipe at age 14. I was getting money from my paper route. Once I left home, I tried just about everything. Things like LSD, mescaline, PCP,[17] cocaine, heroin, and pills. It was kind of funny. I started smoking pot right after they started busing me to another school. I used to be proper, but then they started judging me. It may have to do with segregation. At that time, I didn't know anything about busing and the change may have set me off. I finally ended up getting along with the white guys.

When you got out of high school, how did you get the job at the grocery store?
At first I would meet people in the parking lot and help take their groceries to the car. Doing that, I made my money by tips. After six months the people at the store asked me if I would like a job. I happily accepted. I stayed there for quite a while. The store at first was called Chatham's. Then they were bought out by Tags. And last that I know, they changed the name to Deluxe.

When you worked, where did you stay?
I lived in a house just a couple blocks away. Remember my brother who is in the secret service? I haven't been in touch with him in over 12 years. He lives in Maryland somewhere. Maybe your book will help us get back together. My stepfather died of crack. I've been into crack for years. Earlier he tried to commit suicide by turning on the gas in his apartment. But it didn't matter, the crack ended up killing him.

How often do you use crack and are you on any other drugs?
Once a week I do crack and I take a lot of pills. By the way, I'm not going to give you my last name. If I did that, I would have to kill you.

I'm just kidding. I do have a license to kill. I got it from my brother. I'm just kidding again.

As you got older, how did you get the money for drugs?
They were freebees. People would turn me on to get me started. After that, I did a few B and E's [breaking and entering], but nothing substantial. I got most of my money by helping the man. You know the dealer who sold me stuff. He didn't pay me much, but he was my mentor. He let me stay with him and his wife. I also stayed with his mom and dad. His parents were highly educated people. They were like "Jeopardy" [A TV game show] smart people. Very bright upstairs, but not bright when it came to doing drugs.

How long have you been on the streets?
On and off since the 1970's. I hang around with a lot of white people now. Once I lived in a garage for two years.

Do you panhandle for money?
Sure I do. I sit on some milk crates at the gas station across the street. I ask people if they would like me to pump their gas for a quarter. I've been doing that for 20 years. A lot of people know me. The owner will not tolerate me. But when the owner's brother is there, everything's okay. I keep the parking lot clean and I don't piss the customers off.

I'm going to ask you some questions about drugs. Is that ok?
I'm just the one who can inform you. I'm an expert, but I'm a dummy.

You told me earlier that you do crack cocaine and pills, anything else?
Yes I do, it's called caffeine.

When was the last time you did crack?
About a week ago. When I come down, I take a lot of sleeping pills to get me by. The crack around here is pretty weak. It really doesn't bother me that much, but eventually it's an addiction. I won't deny that.

How does crack make you feel?
It makes me feel euphoric. It's a very unpredictable high. But I know better than to think that the drug can make me feel invincible. Some people take it and feel that they can do anything they fucking want.

Are a lot of people still taking LSD?
I don't know. I have no contact with white dealers anymore.

Can you explain what crack cocaine is?
Its cocaine mixed with baking soda and a little water. You harden it up in a cup. Then you smoke it in a pipe.

What's better, smoking it or snorting it?
Smoking it is better. It gets into your system much faster and it's more euphoric. The drug goes right in to your lungs.

How long does the high last?
Anywhere from 10 to 15 minutes. It makes you wonder why the fuck you're doing it at all.

Do you still smoke marijuana?
Only when I'm bummed out.

Could you work a job right now?
I would be able to work a job.

You really think so?
I know so.

Then why aren't you working?
Because I haven't tried. I would have to get my driver's license renewed. I once drove as a chauffeur. My license was expired but not revoked. The last time it was active was in 2007.

Have you ever gone to prison?
No, but one time I pissed off a couple officers. They caught me with some drugs. I did a bad job of tossing them. They sent me to a city hospital as a mercy gesture. I'm just stupid.

You may be stupid in your decisions, but you seem intelligent when it comes to your vocabulary. What do you think about that?
I'm stupid and belligerent. Some people say I talk like a white man. You got to know when to hold-em, and know when to fold-em. I'm a gambler. My whole life is a gamble and I'm scared to die.

What do you think you're going to die from?
Most likely from drugs. Plus, I don't exercise at all. All I want to do is sleep.

Do you ever go to the doctor?
No, but I need to. I pushed a Q-tip in my ear and plugged it up. Something's in there and I can feel the pressure. I'm going to Dollar General and pick up some wax remover. This bothers me a lot. This is the third time it's happened. I don't want to be deaf at 52 years old.

When you're out on the streets, do you ever get in fights?
I get in altercations. I'm a crummy fighter. I try to avoid it the best I can. Everybody knows me and everyone knows where I live. Who's to say that I may piss someone off one day to where they're going to kill me. Most people know I live alone. I keep my cool and avoid all confrontations. That's called living smart. It's best not to piss somebody off. I don't want to start the O.K. [Old Kindersley] Corral.[18]

Are you on anything right now? You do a lot of drooling.

That's because I don't have any front teeth. It's been a week since I did anything.

But if you were on crack right now, how would you act?

I would be feeling pretty good about myself, but that would be the drug making me feel that way.

What is the worst drug you ever did?

It would be acid. I've had several bad trips. I haven't done that stuff since the 1970's. You know, that drug comes in many forms. It's in pill form, liquid form, and in mushroom form.

Have you ever tried to commit suicide?

I really can't remember. Sometimes when you're on drugs, you don't know what you're doing. But the way I live now, I'm slowly killing myself anyway. Many times I could just walk across the street and I'm not aware of the cars coming. I'm not from Krypton[19] you know. I'm human like everyone else.

Do you ever ask anyone for help?

When I go to church, I may ask the pastor. I went to church pretty steady until they closed a couple months ago. I'm honest you know. I'm honest with everything I'm telling you. What good is going to church and having a relationship with God, if you're going to lie to a pastor. I tell everyone the way it is. In reality, I'm stuck in dreams. There are good dreams and there's drug induced dreams. The drug dreams are nightmares.

You live in the house directly behind the fire station. How did that come about?

The house has been foreclosed. At first, I lived in a car across the street which was in a garage. The people didn't like it much, but they accepted it. Then I moved into the house where I live today. It was foreclosed 12 years ago, and I moved in around four years ago. It has no electricity, gas or water.

How do you go to the bathroom?
I put a plastic bag inside the toilet. When I'm done, it gets thrown out. When I first moved in, the original owner found me. He really didn't care that I lived there. He was a little odd. I once caught him wearing ladies stockings. They were like leotards that you would wear in WWF [World Wrestling Federation]. After a couple years I didn't see him anymore.

Did you ever try getting the water turned on?
Actually I turned it off myself. One winter it got cold and the pipes busted.

Since you're squatting, what would stop someone else from living there?
Good question. It's almost happened a couple times. I don't have a key for the front door, so it's always open. Most people around here know where I live, so they don't bother me. People care about me, but they're not real friends. If I need to use the Internet, I go down to the library. If I have to get washed up, I go down the street to the gas station or the church. I even have a little radio that runs by battery. The one thing I don't like is in the summer time when flies get in my bedroom. They buzz around my head all the time.

Have you ever had a woman in your life?
No I haven't. But if I did, it wouldn't be hard for me to fall in love. For what it's worth, I would rather have a white woman then a black woman. Remember, I'm a black man with a white man's tongue. I'm an outcast amongst my people.

Getting back to your house, how do you see at night?
I have three flashlights. I bought one from Dollar General and the other two I shoplifted.

What is your bed like?
It's the same bed that was in the house when that weirdo left. I also heat the house with a kerosene heater. But this year it smokes, so I can't use it.

So, how do you keep warm?
I stay under the blankets that my neighbors gave me.

I see you're wearing a Detroit firefighter hat. Did a fireman give it to you?
No, I found it in the garbage.

Are there a lot of challenged people in this neighborhood?
Let me tell you a story. About two weeks ago, as I was sitting at the gas station across the street, this lady pulled up in the back and parked her car. She got out and was either drunk or mental. She walked right over to me and sat on my lap. She started rumbling and tumbling around. Then she started complaining to the gas station owner that I took her phone. The next day she came back, but didn't recognize me and I wasn't about to acknowledge her - if you know what I mean.

Where do you get your clothes?
Everything I'm wearing, I found. I check the garbage cans every day.

Where do you get your food?
In the garbage cans. The fire department throws out pretty good food. If the food has spit or bubble gum on it, I just push it off to the side. But if that's all there is, you got to eat. In the summer it's more difficult. I have to beat the maggots to it. I try to look for the fresh food the best I can. The firemen have good food and good cooking skills.

Don't you think it's best to get your driver's license renewed?
The reason I haven't is because I might have a warrant out for my arrest.

What for?
I missed my drops.

What's a drop?
That's when you go to your probation officer and take a pee. There's no reason to go when you're high.

We're just about done, but I want to ask you an unrelated question. Are you Republican or Democrat?
I was born Feb 12th, same as Abraham Lincoln. I was born a Republican.

I want to thank you for your time and here is your $100. Did you still think I wasn't going to give it to you?
It doesn't matter one way or the other. Why don't you just give me a couple dollars?

I don't understand. Why do you only want a couple dollars?
Because $100 will tempt me.

I called Bob back into the room and explained that the man didn't want the $100. So, I gave the fellow $10 and handed Bob the other $90 to hold, and told him that the homeless guy just wanted a little at a time. They both agreed on the arrangement and I headed back home.

Quicksand

"Although homeless can happen to anyone, it just wasn't expected."
Linda Lewis [singer]

Since starting this project, it seemed like the weeks were flying by. One day while driving home after work from the east side of Detroit, I noticed a young Caucasian woman holding a sign. I made a quick U-turn and pulled my car into an old K-mart parking lot. I walked across a busy street, through an uncut grassy divide, and approached the woman. As we stood face to face, she offered her hand with a big smile. She had scraggly, long-blond hair and wore a wool knit cap. I also noticed that she had a considerable amount of dirt under her long untrimmed fingernails. Her face was very withered, probably from a combination of wind and sun. The grime caked on her face reminded me of a young child that had been playing in the dirt all day. Her clothes were worn and soiled to the point of seeing their last days.

After telling her why I was there, she mentioned that she was going to write a book about herself someday. The women asked if I thought it would be a conflict of interest. I replied, "Absolutely not." She continued, "In that case I will be more than happy to tell you anything you'd like to know." She also assured me that everything would be the truth and nothing but the truth. Before leaving she agreed to meet me at 4:00 p.m. the next day on the same corner.

The following day, I picked her up at four o'clock sharp. After getting into my car, she said, "I didn't think you would show up." Asking her why she thought that, her reply was, "It just sounded too good to be true. A hundred dollars is a lot of money."

We decided to eat at a nearby restaurant that specialized in soul food. When we walked in, I asked the lady who greeted us for directions to the rest rooms. She pointed them out and we both went our separate ways. The men's room was nasty. It reminded me of a restroom in an un-kept old southern gas station. She did not finish before me, so I went ahead and picked out a booth in the far corner. More than a few minutes went by and I was starting to wonder whether she had left the restaurant without me noticing. Since the booth was around a corner, I had no direct view of the restrooms. Finally, she found me and apologized for taking so long.

The woman mentioned that she was scrubbing the dirt from under her fingernails. With a shy smile she said, "Sorry, it's been over two weeks since I took a shower." Shortly thereafter, the waiter showed up and asked if we were ready to order. I told her to go first. She turned and asked with a timid voice, "Are you sure I can order whatever I want? You know, I haven't had a steak in about five years." After assuring her that a steak would be fine, she went ahead and ordered. What the heck, it was only $8.99. I told her we would start the interview after the waitress brought our food. Twenty minutes went by and our dinner finally came. Her steak did not look appealing. It was thin and full of gristle. My catfish looked like it would be tasty until I took the first bite. The breading was nice and crispy, but the fish was like mush. One of the side dishes was Mac and Cheese. It looked more like Mac and Sneeze. Also, the green beans had some type of object sticking out from it, which was definitely not edible. It reminded me of a large scale from a carp. Nevertheless, neither of us complained out loud about the food. We began to eat and the interview started.

Could you please tell me your age?
I'm 47 years old.

Were you brought up in any religion?
No, but I baptized myself.

What do you mean?
I grew up across the street from a parochial school. I showed up every day for church and finally joined the school myself. This all started when I was 11 years old.

Do you still follow the Catholic religion?
I consider myself spiritual, but no denomination.

Are your mother and father still alive?
My father died when I was five. He was 30 and died of testicular cancer. My mom remarried right away to my stepfather. He basically raised me. Then he passed away in 2007, but my mother is still alive.

How far did you get in school?
Two years of college.

Do you keep in touch with your mother?
I don't talk to her at all. I'll talk to you later about that.

Was there any abuse growing up?
My mother was an alcoholic and my father smoked pot. It was more like mental abuse. It was always her way.

How long did you live at home?
I lived there up to 18. Then it was on and off till age 20. After that I got married.

Did your mother like the guy you married?
Oh yeah, she liked him a lot.

How long did you stay married?
We're still married. (That's unusual; a homeless married couple.)

Are you together or separated?
Oh no, we're together. (I could see this was going to be an interesting story.) If you want to interview him, I can tell you where he's at.

What does he do for money?
He plays the guitar in front of a strip mall.

Where do you both live?
We're squatting in an abandoned house nearby. We've lived there for three years.

Am I right by thinking that you have no water, electricity or heat?
We have kerosene heat.

When you were married at age 20, was everything good?
Yes, I met the love of my life. We ended up having three children.

How old are they now?
They're 24, 25, and 26. We've been married 27 years. (That was fast work.)

How many boys and girls?
I had two girls and a boy.

How are they doing?
They're doing great. They went to Grand Valley and Michigan State. My one daughter is getting her master's degree.

How often do you talk to your children?
At least once a week. They live far away, so we don't see each other that much.

Do you have a phone?
Yes, I have a phone from the government. We only get 240 minutes a month. Otherwise, I would call my kids every day.

Where did you live right after you were married?
We moved all around at first. Finally, after 10 years we bought a big beautiful home on five and a half acres up north. The house was 2,000 square feet.

Were you and your husband working at that time?
Yes, we both were working at manufacturing companies. I made around $27 an hour and he made about $19 an hour. (That seemed like a pretty good living.)

When did things start going wrong?
The first thing that happened was when my husband and I went swimming at this recreational park. There was this slide that went right into the water. I had this brainless idea that if I poured baby oil all over my body, I would go a lot faster. I had been drinking and I was a little tipsy. When getting to the top, I slipped and snapped my ankle. After having two operations, I stayed in a cast for over a year. At that point the doctors were filling me with all these pain pills. It wasn't a problem until 2007 when my stepfather died. I then ended up getting a DUI. That very much impacted my life. It ruined my whole future. I was humiliated. Then, with all this going on, the company I worked for froze my pay. The recession hit and the automotive companies weren't paying their suppliers. So, because they didn't get paid, neither did we. After 20 years, I ended up losing my job. At the beginning, they sent me to school and everything was great. But after breaking my ankle, losing my job and getting hooked on pain pills, I went into a deep depression. The people I worked with were my best friends. I even have a couple of their names tattooed on my ankle. I know it was just work, but they were like my family. I put my heart and soul into that job. I was a quality

engineer. My mother told me that I would never get anywhere in life. I started working on the floor making $5 an hour and fucking worked all the way up to making $27 an hour. Actually, my husband lost his job first and I ended up carrying all the weight. Then I lost my job. I tried collecting unemployment, but I was denied.

Why were you denied?
Because I couldn't make it into work. With my leg in a cast and being hooked on pills, I was really depressed. I couldn't even leave the house. I was on Vicodin.[20] When it came time to fight for unemployment; I couldn't even stand up for myself. They just fucking denied me on everything. Companies can do that. I didn't do anything wrong. I was just sick. It was the worst time of my life. I couldn't even get my head up off the couch.

At that time, how many kids were still at home?
Just my youngest. He was 17. Our house payment was $1,600 a month and we just couldn't make the payments anymore. We put 35% down, but we ended up with nothing due to a flimflam mortgage company. During that time, they had all these scam type loans. They were going to foreclose on our house, so we went to an attorney. He advised us to file chapter 13. But the one thing he didn't tell us is that we gave up our equity by doing that. It was a bunch of shit. When we walked away from our house, I didn't take a thing. My husband found a job that paid $9 an hour. I have two younger stepsisters and a brother who had the same dad as me. Once my stepdad died, my one sister took care of my mother. My step dad left my mom $250,000. Because of my sister, it was all gone in one year on drugs and alcohol.

How come you didn't get any money?
I had no idea all this was going on. I get a call one day that mom was losing her house.

Where is your sister today?

She just lives down the road. She's a hooker. Her husband's alright with that because of the drugs. That is so messed up. My other ghastly sister found out that my house was vacant, so she drove up north and stole my washing machine. Water ended up leaking all over the floor and completely destroyed everything. That's why I didn't get anything out of the house. Right after we left, my husband and I lived in Detroit. My purse ended up getting stolen. So, between all my personal documents getting destroyed from the flood and my purse ending up gone, I had no identification.

What happened to your mom?

My mom gets $2,500 a month Social Security. She has MS.[21] One day my sister pulls up at her house with a U-Haul and empties everything. She more or less kidnapped her for the use of the inheritance money. Since we were all staying with my mom at that time, we had nowhere to go. Back then, I was hooked on pills and that costs a lot of money.

What happened to your son who was still living with you?

We sent him to live with his aunt. We didn't want him living in Detroit. The aunt lives in the country. I don't want my son in the city. He doesn't need to grow up that way. She took him and there was no problem. Everything was fine.

What happened after that?

I went to jail for a little while.

What for?

After we left my mother's house, my husband and I had nowhere to go, so we stayed in a friend's shed. My sister came one day to visit. She had two little kids and told me that the three of them had no place to live. So, I let them stay in the shed with us. The neighbors saw what was going on, so they called the police. I ended up getting a ticket for contributing to the delinquency of minors. So, I got six months in jail.

What about your sister?
She got in a lot more trouble than me. They put her on a tether because of the children, but she ended up cutting it off.

Previously, you said that the pills were expensive. How did you pay for them?
I didn't. At that time heroin was everywhere and it was cheap. The doctors kept prescribing me pills. Then one day they say, "No more." You can't do that to people. Something has to be done with the doctors and drug companies. They keep you going and then they cut you off. Now I'm hooked on heroin. Can you believe I didn't get hooked on heroin until I was 41 years old?

When you had to get out of the shed, where did you go?
This house down the street was in foreclosure and we kept an eye on it. Since no one claimed it, we moved in. All the neighbors love us. In fact, the neighbor across the street said if he could afford to buy it, he would give it to us. They became real good friends. Every couple weeks, they let us take a shower over their house. They know what the deal is. We're just normal people who got caught up in the system.

How did you get started on heroin?
As I was trying to get off the pills, I started to get very sick. I needed something to get me through the pain. So my sister, who's the prostitute, got me into it.

Is your husband on heroin?
Yes he is. Day after day I would bitch to him how good it was. One day, I finally talked him into it and he loved it.

Were you scared the first time you used it?
Not at all. I read so much about it; the process was easy for me. I shot it up the first time and I felt great. Ten years ago I would have never even

thought of it, but because of the whole pill thing, it wasn't a problem. You just want to do anything to get away from reality.

How long have you been on heroin?
It's been around six years now.

How many times do you shoot up a day?
Three times a day.

I interviewed a girl a while back who said that she's been on heroin for six years. She told me her habit costs $30 a day. Does that sound about right?
Are you kidding, not at all. At the very least it's costing her between $75 and $100 a day.

How many drug dealers have you gone through in the last six years?
We've used the same one all these years. He's very good. Before he puts it out on the streets, he has me sample it first. I trust him because he cuts it with vitamin B and that's good for you. (How can you say a drug is better for you because it is mixed with a vitamin?)

Does the dealer have another job?
Why would he need another job? He makes plenty of money doing that. His kids go to private school. He owns five houses and he has a ton of cars. Young kids come to him all the time for drugs, but he's not into that.

Would you mind telling me his race?
He's black, but was brought up in a very high-end white neighborhood.

Do you ever have problems getting it?
Just recently my dealer went down for a couple weeks.

What does that mean?
He ran out. He had to go out of state to get it.

I thought it was so plentiful. Why did he run out?
I have no idea. So anyway, we had to get our stuff elsewhere. It was just hell. We went to strange places and met strange people. It was pretty scary. We became real good friends with our dealer. I remember one time he told my husband, "We have to get your wife off this shit." My husband didn't want me off because he didn't want to get off himself. That's how sick the mind works of a drug user. Let's face it, the drug dealer wants my money.

When you panhandle, how much money do you collect?
It depends. The worst day was $7 and the best day was $300, but $300 is rare. I've been out here for three years and there is this one gentleman who gives me $150 every time with no questions asked. He doesn't come by that often, but when he does I get $150.

This is kind of an odd question, but why do you stand on a corner that doesn't do very good?
Because I feel guilty even doing it now. The traffic light only lasts nine seconds. So when people hand me money, they really have to work fast. During the summer I'm not out panhandling. I have a lawn mower and I cut lawns in the neighborhood. I can make 100 bucks a day doing that.

Earlier you told me that your husband plays the guitar for money. Do you pool your money together?
Not at all. Whatever money he gets, he uses for his drugs and the money I get, I use for my drugs.

Do your children know you're on heroin?
Yeah they all know, but we're going to quit soon. We're going to be grandparents.

You're going to quit, just like that?
It's not going to be that easy, but with the new baby coming, it will give us a good reason to quit. I can't do it for myself, but I can do it for the baby.

Has your husband agreed to this?
He sure has, but it's not going to be easy. Neither of us have ID, so it would be hard to check in somewhere for rehab. We have no insurance and when we do get clean, I don't want to be on methadone.[22] I want to be completely clean. If you stay on methadone, you'll never get clean. My husband and I keep talking about it. We first said, "By the time the baby's born we're going to quit." Now we say, "By the time the baby walks we're going to quit." When I told my daughter what we were going to do, she cried. I knew it affected her, but I didn't know how much. I thought since they're living their own lives, they really didn't care. I was wrong. I remember last Christmas. My daughter made a snide remark to my son, "See that woman over there. She was once your mother." She got her dig in.

What does your sign read?
It reads, "Homeless, hungry, need water, double A and D batteries, socks, and books."

Does your husband have any other jobs?
Yes, he does odd jobs up and down the strip. He comes home from work at night and goes to bed. In the morning he gets straight and off to work he goes.

Does getting straight mean getting high?
Yes.

Through my experience from past interviews, I found the best place to panhandle is in the suburbs. Why don't you go there?
Like I said, I'm embarrassed. I'll just stay in Detroit.

Getting back to the heroin. After six years of using, do you still get high?

It's not what it was like when you first do it, but you still get high.

What's the high like?

It's really hard to explain. It's wonderful. You get this warm feeling from the back of your neck to your head, and all your pain and troubles leave your body. It just makes you feel good. It makes you smile. Once there was this little nerd boy who came up to me and asked if I would help him shoot up for the first time. I was so excited for him because I knew what he was going to experience. That's the mentality of a drug user. I did that for him because it's so unbelievable. I really don't want anybody to start it, but just to watch someone get high for the first time is great.

Didn't you feel like his life was ruined at that point?

Not really. He was already hooked on Fentanyl. Heroin was just a better drug. My mother is on Fentanyl patches because of her MS. My sister steals it from her and shoots it right into her own veins. I would never do anything like that. My husband and I keep very clean. We don't have Hep C or HIV.

These drugs are pretty scary. Do you know many other people on them?

You have no idea. Many of the big wigs like CEOs, and so on, are hooked too. They just cover it up. The one good thing, that's good, is that the "non-users" are starting to change. They don't treat us like criminals anymore. You can go to any pharmacy and buy needles with no questions asked.

Let me tell you a story while it's on my mind. There is this guy who is a pastor at our church in Detroit. Someone gave him a badge, so he goes around frisking everyone. I saw him frisk this 16 year old kid. I told him, "You can't do that." Ever since I told him that, he's out to get me. He knows I have a drug problem. He follows me everywhere. I'm not imagining it. This is how sick he is. He knows a lot of drug dealers, but leaves them alone. Here is what he does. He has actual dealers try to sell me drugs, so he can call the undercover cops. Money has to change hands to get arrested. I won't do that. It's amazing how the undercover cops drive around in their old trucks or old beater cars just to pick you up. Last Good Friday that pastor tried to set us up. He had the Narc Squad in a big van outside my house. We're not big drug dealers. We're just a couple of everyday users. He had cops watching us, but nothing happened. I've been running from this man for one year now. He knocks on neighbors' doors and flashes this fake badge. He tells them that they got to get us out of the neighborhood. He's not even a cop. Everybody who lives in the neighborhood knows us, but some people just want to jump on his band wagon. You could write a whole chapter on just how bizarre this guy is.

It seems to me that between the money you collect and the side jobs your husband has, you would have a lot of money left over. What do you do with the extra?
Every bit of it goes towards drugs. I'm $100 a day and my husband is more. But like I said, we keep our habits separate. He's greedy when it comes to drugs. Again, that's the mentality of a drug user. As time goes on, you use more and more. If he's low on money, I will help him out. When you buy, you get one for $20, two for $35, and three for $50. We always get three for $50 to save money. I usually do one or two in the morning, one or two in the afternoon, and try to do three at night. They say on the news that heroin is cheap, it's not. When your tolerance goes up, your use goes up.

Do you think heroin turns people into thieves?
No I don't. I believe once a crook always a crook. I never stole anything. Everybody takes care of their habit in a different way. Drug users tell me the best way to get money is credit card fraud. I can't do

that. To me, that's outright stealing. If someone wants to give me money, that's okay. They passed a law in Detroit, as long as you're not panhandling in front of an ATM or restaurant, you're good to go. It gives you something to do all day and I meet a lot of great people doing that. Deep down inside, I hate doing this. What if they found out?

Who are they?
The kind people who gave me money. What if they found out I do heroin? They just don't know. I don't look like the stereotypical person who does drugs.

I'm going to ask you what I consider an unusual question. When you shoot up, do you always use the same place on your body?
No I don't. But you know, years ago they used a much thicker needle. That's why back then you would see a bunch of needle tracks going up and down their arms. Today, it's a fine little prick and hardly leaves a mark at all. But I will tell you this; you have to rotate your shots. If you don't, your vein will collapse. You will kill it. My sister has tattoos all over her body. You could never tell on her.

Your sister - is she married?
No, but she lives with a sugar daddy. He can't support her habit, so he lets her prostitute.

How old is your sister?
She's 36.

Why doesn't she get off the street and get a job as a dancer?
She's too old for that. She did that at a younger age. I believe she made pretty good money too. I wish she wouldn't sell her body. She's been selling herself ever since she lived with my mom. It's been a long time. When my sister was stealing my mother's Fentanyl patches, they had to be replaced. So, my mother justified my sister selling her body. I just don't get it. I left the house at an early age to get away from that type of

thinking. My sister told me she has been raped many times, but she's a big liar. She's a psychopath.

You said all your money is for drugs. What about the other things you need?

This is what I do. I have one pocket for drugs and I have the other pocket for necessities. You have to have certain items to live, but here's the thing. I don't need to buy a lot. People give me food, clothes, soap, and just about anything I would need to live. The people you see out there with nasty shoes and nasty clothes, they're the fakers. (When I first saw her, she looked nasty.)

There's this girl who sets up about a mile away. She is dressed up so nasty, but she lives in a beautiful house with her husband. The ones who look destitute are usually just fine. They collect more money than the ones who really need it. You get good clothes from people or your local church. You don't need to look destitute. For God's sake, people even give you baby wipes. You don't need that dirt on your face.

Why do you have dirt under your fingernails?

We don't have running water. I tried scrubbing them the best I could in the bathroom, but I didn't have anything to get up under the nails.

How dirty is it in your house?

I do the best I can to keep the cobwebs out, but it's still pretty bad. I also try to disinfect it to the best of my ability. We have a couch, a chair, and a kerosene heater. One thing I do to save a lot of money is I pick up cigarette butts. I won't buy cigarettes. I pick them up in front of stores and gas stations. If I find a long one, I get all excited. When I went to jail, I had to give up both heroin and cigarettes. One was just as hard to give up as the other, except with heroin you get sick. When I was in jail, it was hell. I was sick for three weeks. I didn't eat at all. You have to quit cold turkey and there's nothing they will do for you. All I thought about the whole time was dying. After I got out, I went right back to shooting up.

Then how are you going to quit when your grandbaby comes?
I know what you're saying. It's going to be hard. If one of us doesn't want to quit, then it most likely won't happen. There was this one rehab place in Detroit where the judge sent me. It was crazy. All they wanted to do was give you pills which sent you off into la la land. You didn't care about anything. Then they moved me to a rehab in Romulus, Michigan. I escaped from there. I waited till the guard wasn't looking in the courtyard and I just walked out.

What's your husband's personality like?
He's very outgoing, but also very passive. He's a good guy. Before we were married, we were just friends. We would get drunk and kissed for hours. It wasn't till later that we became lovers.

When you and your husband get off the drugs, will both of you need a job? Won't that be hard?
Believe me; standing on a corner all day is much harder than working. I love to work, but with my habit it's not possible. It's not the standing there that bothers me. I've had shit and urine thrown at me. They will also throw apples and money at me. Whatever they can get their hands on. People drive by holding their nose. They're showing me that I stink. I believe the people who do this are the people who have been teased all their lives. It's a way of getting back. Some people are just cruel. People stop all the time and take my picture. Then they end up posting me on social media. It's just like you're an animal in a zoo. It's creepy as hell when someone just walks up to you and takes your picture. It takes everything in me just to go out and beg. I grew up in this area and once they posted me on social media. I have a lot of gawkers from high school who will show up. I don't care for any of those people anyway.

Let me tell you what happened. When I was a senior in high school, I got in a bad car accident. My car was T-boned on the passenger side by a truck. My best friend died and I've been carrying that with me ever since. The kids at school were so cruel. They called me "killer" and names like that. The authorities wanted to get me on involuntary manslaughter, but the judge threw it out of court. I loved my friend, but the kids in school were just garbage to me. I was 17 and when you're that age people just don't care.

Why don't you try to get a part time job?
Look at me. It's been 19 days since I took a shower. Would you want to work next to me? They use to let me shower at the YWCA, but they closed it. And those Swedish spas, they're like $25 an hour. I can't afford that. Those rooms are nasty anyway.

What can be nastier, those showers or you not washing up for over two weeks.
You don't get it. Those showers are really nasty.

Can't you get a little extra money to clean up?
I am so embarrassed standing on that corner. Once I get enough money for my drugs, I'm done. This one boy stopped and said, "Ever since I started giving you money, my whole life has changed." I feel happy for him, but I still don't like panhandling. I'm not stupid. I know this is bad for my body, but I've lived a very healthy life up to six years ago. I understand that I have an addictive personality which was handed down from my family. My grandmother was an alcoholic and my mother's an alcoholic. At one time I drank every day, but not to any extent. I realize that once I'm off the heroin, I will still have to fight every day for the rest of my life. The urge will never leave me. Not everyone is affected by opiates$_{23}$ or alcohol the same way, but I have that addictive personality. I warn my kids about it all the time. All my children drink socially. I tell them, "Watch it." They all smoke too. Damn it, I tell them

not to smoke, but they don't listen. Did you know in Canada they will give you heroin in almost any clinic? (I didn't know if that was true or false.) Look how hard I have to work every day to keep my habit. There's a lot of ingenuity going on with me. I hate it, but I love it.

What do you love about it, besides the way it makes you feel?
I'm out of society. We're off the grid. Plus, it stops me from committing suicide.

What is the biggest side effect from heroin?
It's when you overdose. I OD'd twice.

How do you OD?
You have to remember, they step on it four or five times before it gets to you. That's why you try to stick with the same dealer. You never know what other dealers are going to add to it.

You told me that your dealer was good, so how did you OD?
When I got out of jail, I went right back to the amount I was using before I went in. It works the same way for an alcoholic. One time my sister shot me up while I was drinking. I died that day and the doctors brought me back to life.

Do you or your husband get any assistance from the government?
We get nothing and I don't want anything. All I need right now is enough to live on. People have their choice. Pay me out of your pockets or pay me out of your taxes. I prefer their pockets. It's a lot cheaper that way. What I don't like is the motherfucker who collects disability and also panhandles at the same time. What do you think about those people on crack? Now that's a cheap drug. Those people will dig up their dead grandmother out of the ground and pull out their gold teeth. I know most of those people out there can't work, but I'm dying to work. I don't care if I'm on heroin or not. I'll do just about any kind of job. There's no doubt that I could become a functioning heroin addict.

There are so many people out there in the working force that are on heroin. It would make your head spin.

From the first time you shot up, how long did it take before you were addicted?

Right away. Remember, I was already addicted to pills. I could have had a whole different life. With a combination of the right medicine and some good therapy, things could have been way different. Just so you know, my habit hasn't changed in the last four years. I have hit a plateau.

What did your husband say about this meeting of ours?

He was a little nervous. I was supposed to text your license plate to him, but as I see now there's no need. Neither one of us knew what was going to happen. Remember, $100 is a lot of money. And just so you know, I'm a big reader and I have a lot of respect for you. At least this way, you'll let the readers know what goes on in the real world. Plus, it will make young people think twice before they go ahead and do something stupid.

I was eating dinner last night with my daughter and she was scared knowing you were going to get into my car. Do you understand her fear?

I'm a girl. I should be more scared getting in a man's car. Believe it or not, when you picked me up, I had a couple people watching out for me. There are a lot of good people out there. They just wanted to make sure I was safe. Let me also say this. When you offered me $100 for my story, I felt you weren't giving it to me. It was more like I was earning it.

Let me ask you this. If I didn't offer you money, would you still tell me your story?

I don't think anyone would talk to you, but the way you're doing it there's no way they wouldn't.

Do you feel that people should care what you do with the money they give?
It's none of their business. If you're going to give me money in the first place, why should you even care? If you do care, then why give any. Once I leave here, I am going to spend a dollar on a newspaper.

We finished eating and after paying the bill I offered to take her home, but she preferred to walk. So, we ended up going our separate ways.

This interview was very interesting to me. Her story had much more detail than the others. Not only that, I left with a better understanding of what a long-time heroin addict faces.

The Bitch

"The world of the homeless is a tough and interesting world."
Paul Dano [actor]

A few more weeks went by and my friend Marty told me about this great sale at JC Penny. Marty is like a blood hound that can sniff out every rock bottom sale in the area. He told me, "Don't wait too long or everything will be gone." So, the next morning I drove to JC Penny arriving at 10:00 a.m. sharp, and purchased the last five men's winter coats. They normally sold for $100 each, but I snapped them up for $6.50 apiece. I think the reason they didn't sell previously was because they were red. But what the heck, the way I figured it, the homeless wouldn't care anyway.

Saturday came and I headed back to downtown Detroit. My plan was to pass out a few coats and pick up an interview at the same time. While driving through this one area that had a few stores and bars strung together, I noticed an African American woman. She was tucked up under some thick woolly blankets, trying to keep warm. Although it was early May, the high that day was projected to be 47°F and the wind was quite brisk.

I parked the car, approached her from the side, and asked if she would be willing to tell her life story for my book. She shouted with her arms flailing back and forth, "I will do it under one condition." I thought, "I hope it's nothing too drastic." Wearing my standard smile, I asked, "And what would that be?" She replied, "You must use my name in your story." I explained that it would be impossible because of privacy reasons. After a hardy laugh she said, "Not my real name. Around here I'm known as 'The Bitch'." Before I could continue the conversation, four rough looking dudes started to surround me. I wasn't sure what they were thinking or what they might do, so I acted quickly and said, "You guys look cold. Would anyone like a brand new coat?" If anything bad was going to happen, it was instantly diffused. We walked over to my car and I passed out the coats one by one. It almost looked like I just created a gang. They could call themselves, "The Red Coat Boys." Now that everyone seemed happy, it was time to start the interview.

Just then, one of the guys asked me if I had any paper towels or baby wipes in the car. After which he started jumping up and down crying out, "I have to take a dump." I reached into my car and retrieved an old towel that was used during the last golf season. It was all I had and certainly was better than nothing. He was more than happy and disappeared behind an old dumpster next to the side of a nearby building. The woman remarked, "My brother really appreciates that." I exclaimed, "You mean that's your brother?!" She then spun around and pointed at the other three guys, "Yeah and those are my cousins. They always stand around protecting me." I pointed at the dumpster and asked, "Is that where everyone goes to the bathroom?" She explained that if there are no bathrooms available, the dumpster was the emergency spot. She continued, "By the way, behind that dumpster it is cleaner than most of the bathrooms that we use at the local restaurants." I asked if she would like to sit in my car for the interview. She agreed, so we began.

What is your age?
I'm 34.

What is your nationality?
Half black and half white. I'm African American and Cherokee Indian.

When you were born, were your parents married?
They were living together, but not married.

Were you brought up in any religion?
My mother was Jehovah witness, but I never converted.

Do you follow any religion now?
I'm Baptist.

Does your mother and father still live together?
My father was murdered when I was six.

Can you tell me what happened to your father?
It's hard for me to talk about it. My father was a big drug lord. Someone owed him some money. When he couldn't pay, my father turned around to reach for his shot gun and the guy shot my dad in the back. I was standing right there when it happened.

Where was your mother?
She was in the kitchen. I don't want to talk about that anymore. It's a memory you can never shake. It keeps playing over and over in my head. My mother put me in therapy at that early age, but it really didn't help.

(She then put her hands over her eyes and started to cry.)

Would you consider that was one of your downfalls?
It was the only downfall that put me where I am today. We lived very well up to that point. I could have whatever I wanted. My father spoiled me, but after that day I turned mean. One day I lit the house on fire. I would constantly fight and cause trouble.

When your father died, how did your family get money?
My mother got Social Security until I was 25.

How far did you get in school?
I made it to 11th grade with honors. I was ready to attend Eastern University.

What happened?

I met a man and lost my virginity. I lost my school and I lost my mind.

What do you mean?

I left everything for this man. He was a drug dealer too. He gave me whatever I needed. I kept the same pattern that I received from my father.

Did you have any children?

I had two children by him. My youngest and oldest are from him.

How many children do you have in all?

I have seven all together. My first man was always trying to control me. He would say, "Oh, you're so good with children, you should have been a teacher." I'm a free spirit. I want to do what I want to do.

Let's go back a little bit. What happened from age six to seventeen?

When I was 13, I started selling crack.

Back then, how much money were you making?

Between $300 to $400 a day. I would sell double-ups.

What does that mean?

Everything I sold, I would double up the cost. I would always pay for my dope ahead of time. If you don't do that, you could get in trouble. One day my mama found some dope in my room and she said, "What are you doing? Are you trying to be like your daddy?" She was mad and demolished my room. She then told me if I want to be like my daddy, I need to help pay the bills. Once I started doing that, everything was cool. (It's amazing how people rationalize a situation.)

Did you work a normal job during that time?

I used to clean seats at the old Tiger Stadium. Even though I was making good money selling drugs, I wanted to make more. That's why I had a job. At age 16, I was able to buy a car and a house. I was making lots of money. I wanted to be on top. I felt good on top. I did whatever it took to make money. I wanted to be my own boss.

So what happened?
Here come the police. I got busted. But even in jail, if you got the right connections, you can make good money there too. Drugs cost much more in jail. A nickel bag [$5 worth of drugs] out here would cost you $30 behind bars. Then I got caught selling a second time and had to go back again.

How long were you in for?
Not long. Each time was a misdemeanor. I'm not stupid. It would be a felony if you're caught with a large quantity. These niggas out here just don't think. What you do is put your entire mother fuckin crack in one bag. If you keep them in individual bags, it makes them hard to ditch when the police come. You can flush that shit quickly. These niggas are stupid. I haven't sold dope in years you know. It was way simpler back in the 80s. Today, these people are stupid. Then some niggas say, "My product is better than yours." People wake up! The product sells itself.

Getting back to the man you fell in love with and had two children. How old were you?
I was 17, but let's get something straight. I didn't fall in love with him. I fell in love with his money. He had plenty of money. He got me with champagne and a bear skin rug. You would never catch me drinking beer. I was always drinking champagne. I was living the life. I left him after a year and had two more kids by another man. Then I came back. I had three more kids from the third guy.

Out of the seven kids, how many do you keep in touch with?
I talk to all of them. They all have foster parents. The foster parents are very nice. All my kids are doing well.

Did you ever consider birth control?
I did for a while, but all my hair started falling out. I won't take those things anymore.

Can you still get pregnant?
No, I got my tubes tied. I don't do diapers anymore.

How did you lose all your kids?
Child protection services took them away.

Who called them?
I called them myself. I wanted my babies taken care of.

Before your kids were taken, how did you live?
I was living in a two bedroom house. I made money by making dinners for the neighbors. Each night I charged them $10 a plate. That was a good hustle. I cooked my ass off. Sometimes my neighbors would bring their friends. No one messed with me in the kitchen. My specialties were steak, beef ribs, and macaroni and cheese. Trust me. I'm the one you want cooking in the kitchen. Nobody can cook as well as me. I learned from my big mama.

Is your mother still alive?
Yes, but I don't know where she lives. She's paranoid schizophrenic with homicidal tendencies. (That's a mouth full.)

So, she doesn't see her grandkids?
I don't want her nowhere near my kids. She would always beat my ass for no reason. I don't want her touching them.

Have you ever been in any psychiatric wards?
No, but when I get mad, it's time for you to back off. I don't care who you are, no one messes with me. As long as you respect me, I'll respect you.

Do you use drugs now?
I haven't done drugs in eight years. I'm just a bad alcoholic. I might hit a blunt every once in a while, but that's about it.

How much do you drink a day? Would you say a fifth?
A fifth? That's what I drink for breakfast. The alcoholics are cool around here. If you're a drug user, I don't want anything to do with you. All I want to do is drink and be happy.

Getting back to your kids, are you allowed to see them?
Every Tuesday. There's no case against me. The judge was mad. She said, "So, this is a case of poverty?" Even though I drink, I was a good mother. I love my kids. I would do anything for them. Wherever I go, kids flock to me. I love to love my kids. My life is just fucked up.

You told me that you had an uncontrollable temper. What about when it comes to your kids?
Why would I lay a hand on the kids? I love my kids.

But you were abused. How come that anger wasn't passed on to you?
Why would someone raise their kids in such a way, if you didn't like it yourself? If you didn't like being abused, then why in the hell would you abuse someone else? That's stupid. I have made a lot of mistakes in my life. I screwed up my scholarship to Eastern University. I screwed up picking the wrong man, but I'm not going to screw up my kids. I fucked up my life, but I won't do that to my kids. I will whoop their ass for one reason and one reason only. That's if they don't walk the straight and narrow. I don't want them to end up the way I did. Their foster parents are so sweet. I love them. The foster mother asked me if it was ok for my kids to call her grandma. Hell yes, it's ok. My son said, "Hey mom, grandma took us to Ducky Cheese." I thought, "What the hell is Ducky Cheese." As I'm sure you know, he meant Chucky Cheese. I'm blessed.

I couldn't take care of all my kids. God sent me these angels to take care of my babies until I can get them back.

Has anything unusual ever happened in your life?
When I was 25, I hit a tree with my car. I was in a coma for two weeks. They had to pry the car apart to get me out. I was drunk driving. While in the hospital, I felt a hand lay right on my chest. That's what brought me out of the coma. It was a blurred vision, but a quick vision of somebody all in white. I was good after that. I believe that was the hand of God. That was the turning point in my life. My faith became strong, and I stopped drugs.

Do you have any remaining problems from the coma?
I have bad headaches and insomnia. If I don't drink, I can't sleep.

Where do you get your money for alcohol?
From begging on corners.

Do you have a sign?
Yes I do. It says, "God Bless the Homeless." I do my best on opening day of baseball season. There's no reason you should be broke on opening day.

Where are you living now?
Right against the building where you found me.

Why don't you live in the shelters?
They're too dirty. It's much cleaner on the sidewalk.

How do you keep warm?
Blankets and hand warmers. I've been out here a whole year.

Does the church help?
They gave me a one bedroom apartment, but what am I going to do with a one bedroom? To get my kids back, I have to get a place that has

a bedroom for each kid. I also have to show a steady income. I might as well just stay on the street till I get a place with enough rooms, so I can get my kids back.

How long has it been since you had your kids?
It's been one year and a couple months. Living out on the streets, I don't get to cook anymore. When I had a house full of kids, I would make a big pot of spaghetti. I don't know how to cook for just one individual. Thinking about how I used to be with my family wants to make me cry.

Don't you think the main reason you're out on the streets is because of your drinking?
Sure it is, but I drank the whole time while raising my children. When I get my kids back, there shouldn't be a problem. The authorities know about my drinking. Since there is no case of abuse, I will get them back. On the record, I gave up my kids because of poverty. Since that's the only thing against me, I should be able get them back.

Can you keep a job as an alcoholic?
I can, but only for a few hours a day. Ever since my car accident, I get tired very easy. This week for the first time, I'm starting to have seizures. I've been to the hospital twice. They have yet to put me on any medicine. I really need to get a house for my babies. If a crack-head can get a house why can't I? Maybe I should start smoking crack. Right now I get no assistance. The only thing I get is a bridge card and a phone. They have resubmitted my package for the housing program, but it's a long drawn out process. They say it could be up to six months before they review my files. [A Michigan Bridge Card is used to purchase certain food products and access cash benefits at a number of retailers and ATMs throughout the state.]

How will they contact you when it's time?
All my information is with the church.

You seem very clean for a street person. Where do you wash?

I can go to the local churches. I just go in the bathroom and wash up. Once a week they let you wash your clothes. If I can't get in the church, I'll wash up at Subway.

I noticed your teeth are very white. How do you keep them so nice?

I'm not sure. I guess they're naturally like that. Every morning I bend over a trash can with a toothbrush and a bottle of water. I can't be dirty. It just doesn't feel right. I've always been clean. Homelessness does not determine your character. Homelessness means you do not live in a home and nothing else. It doesn't mean that you urinate on yourself or take drugs. You don't have to be dirty, stinky or smelly. I love myself. A lot of these people out here have mental problems, but at the end of the day you still have to love yourself.

Where do you take a pee?

I got baby wipes. It's usually behind a dumpster or a large sign.

What if you have to go number two?

I go right in a garbage can. It's usually pretty clean. If a restaurant or a church is not open, you use what's ever available to you. When you got to go, you got to go. I may also use a clean alley. With baby wipes and hand sanitizer, you're good to go.

When you're panhandling, what happens if you don't get enough money for the day?

I really don't need much. Give me enough money for a bottle and I'm happy. Twenty dollars gets you a bottle and a pack of Newport's.

Other than your seizures, do you have any other health problems?

I only have one lung. I lost my other one from the car accident. I guess I shouldn't smoke.

Do you follow politics?
Out on the street I know everything that goes on. That's why I don't vote. If I did vote, I would vote independent. Politics are all crooked. That's the biggest dope game in the world. I can get deep into that subject. They don't give me no money. It's a bunch of rich motherfuckers sitting around a table. It's the big pockets against the little pockets. That's why I don't even fool with it, but if you put my ass in charge for one month without drinking, everything would be all right. Let me give you an example of what I would do. You pay a nigga hundreds of thousands of dollars to shoot hoops. Do you know how many people that could feed?

Talking about food, how do you get your food?
We either get it from church or when people bless us with food. But if food gets short, we all ante up and go to the store.

I noticed when I first walked up; you seemed to have control of the people standing around you. Does everyone listen to you?
You better believe it. I'm the queen bee around here. I'm the top bitch. I had a friend once tell me, "You're good for two things, making pretty babies and cooking your ass off." You know what? I'll accept that.

Are you ever afraid out in the streets?
Hell no. I have security all around me. I like being the queen bee. My brother and cousins out here protect me. They're all alcoholics too.

Do you think your brother can work?
My brother is so damn slow. He has nothing when it comes to brains. All he knows how to do is whoop ass. He was working in the church making $10 an hour, but he got in a bad fight one day and they fired him. It pissed me off that they fired him because the fight took place after hours. A nigga pulled a knife on him, so he whooped his ass. He was just protecting himself. They should have fired him because of all the flirting he did. He would hit on any type of woman. I don't care if

they're white, black, fat or skinny. He loves them all. He could have been fired for that, but they fired him for whipping a nigga's ass. He did a WWF on that nigga. He picked him up and dropped him over his knee.

Did he get arrested?
Hell no, we don't snitch on each other. We're our own police.

What ever happened to the guy with the knife?
He still hangs around here. He's crazy, but he won't mess with my brother again. It makes me mad because that $10 an hour job is gone. But some people in the church are trying to get him back. That's bull shit, firing a nigga for protecting himself.

I was told by another homeless person out here that most people have knives and don't carry guns. Is that true?
Yes, that is true. Let me tell you why. It's known amongst us that if you try to protect yourself with a gun, you're not much of a man. It takes a man to carry a knife and not a gun. It takes a real nigga to only carry a knife. I carry a knife if I have to fight a man, but if I have to fight a woman I hit her with these. (She held up her fists to show me.) Down here they call me, "Stabalina." That's just what they call me. I'm really an angel. I don't start anything. I just make sure to finish it.

A few weeks ago I drove around the corner and there were hundreds of people living in the shelters. Is it dangerous around there?
Stay away from there, if you value your life. If you look like you could be had, you will either get raped, robbed, choked or whatever the fuck else they want to do. If they see they can get you, they will, and you will not see it coming. I was living there with my kids for a while, but it's not the place to be. If you go over there, it's like going into a jungle. I'm just glad I have a sperm donor over there, so I'm good. I ain't got nothin to worry about. That's my old stomping ground around there.

Getting back to your sleeping place next to the building. How do you keep warm when it gets real cold?
We know how to do it. First, we lay down plastic. Then we lay down cardboard. Then I have an old sleeping bag and last, I cover myself up with a couple blankets. After that, you're good to go. I also use hand warmers, but I burned myself pretty bad. You have to be careful when you're drunk. One night I got all warm and toasty in my sleeping bag, so I started stripping off all my clothes. Those hand warmers really burnt the shit out of me.

I have to ask you this. Are you drunk right now?
Yes, I'm drunk. With all long time alcoholics, it's hard to tell. Your body eventually gets use to it. You just act normal, but if you notice I'm pretty healthy. I like to pump myself with good stuff. I eat good food and drink a lot of water.

How long have you been drinking alcohol?
Since I was two years old. When my daddy wasn't looking I drank his beer, but I seriously started drinking when I was 13.

Would you like to stop drinking?
Not really. Drinking's not my issue. What I would like to stop is smoking those nasty cigarettes. It's hard to believe, but I'm smoking with one lung. I live day to day. Whatever happens, happens. You see, the white people screwed up. If they would have just left us in Africa, I would be living in my own country and not living on the streets. Where's the help. No one is doing anything for me. I had a job where I made $8 an hour, but you can't live on $8 an hour. A lot of people like to take advantage of people like me. Eight dollars an hour ain't shit.

I have one more question. How do you see your future?
I just want to get a house and have my babies back. It's going to be a tough road, but if anyone can do it, I can.

Once again, I left an interview with my head spinning in thought. So many people get in an unwanted situation by little fault of their own. You might say that this woman had choices, but those choices were few when it came to the type of upbringing she had as a child.

The Forgotten Veteran

"When passerby's ignore homeless people, they don't know if that was a man or woman in uniform previously. They should not be invisible. They cannot be ignored."
Max Martini [actor]

It was now the end of May and the weather was starting to warm up. During a past conversation with a homeless man, I was told about a veteran who was caught up in the system. He resided in a state subsidized nursing home with no way out. It wasn't that he needed constant help; he just had no place to go. Wanting to get his story, I drove to the home and asked for directions to his room. There, lying in a bed was a man with a long unmanaged beard and grey hair dangling past his shoulders. To the left of him, sitting on a portable food table, were a dozen or so books. Without expecting much cooperation, I introduced myself and asked if he would participate in an interview. From past experiences, I found it very difficult to find any veteran who was willing to talk. But once he understood the purpose of my visit, he agreed that his story must be told.

The nursing home was a very low-end facility. As I was taking a seat, his dinner came. He lifted up the brown plastic cover revealing his food. All I can say is that it was unrecognizable. On the plate were two hard yellow squares of something. Next to them were a scoop of white and a hunk of green. I asked if he was on a special diet. Very angrily he replied, "How the hell would I know? No one talks to me here." I took my recorder, laid it next to him on the bed, and asked if he would like to eat dinner first. He exclaimed, "Hell no, I'm not going to eat this shit!" He shoved the food off to the side and I began asking questions.

May I ask how old you are?
I'm 72. My birthday was three days ago.

What can you tell me about your mother and father?
I'm adopted. I was six days old when they took me from the hospital.

Did you ever meet your real mother and father?
No.

Did your adopted mother and father stay married while you were growing up?
No, I really had no use for my mother at all. She wore the pants in the family. She wouldn't let me do anything. If I went and asked my father for something, he would say, "Go ask your mother." That would upset me to no end. I would say to my father, "You're my dad. Why can't you make the decisions in the family?" My mother messed my brother up so bad, he ended up gay. I remember one year my mother bought my brother a three foot tall doll for Christmas. Who does stuff like that? My mother divorced my dad. He worked seven days a week. I think the only reason he worked that much was to get away from her. She did everything possible to hurt him. Every chance my mother had, she would take that opportunity.

How old were you when they got divorced?
I was 11 or 12. Unfortunately, I had to live with my mother. My brother was allowed to do anything, but she was tough on me. That's why I left home.

Were you brought up in a religion?
My father was Catholic, but when he married my mother, she made him leave the church. They tried bringing up my brother and me as Protestants, but I didn't go for it. They would send me and my brother to church, but yet they didn't go. The way I looked at it, if they're not going, then I'm not going. I would leave for church on Sunday and not come back till it was over. They would ask me how church was and I would say, "It was a good service."

How far did you get in school?
I made it to the 10th, and that's when I left home. I went to the race track with thoroughbred horses. I worked there and lived there.

How long did you work there?
On and off about 35 years.

Tell me the story of how you ended up in the service?
When I was 17, I got kicked by a horse. The doctors would not work on me without consent. My dad signed the papers and I had the operation. The horse kicked me right in the ball sack, so I needed to get it repaired. Then as soon as I was 18, I enlisted in the Navy. The accident I had with the horse didn't stop them from accepting me.

Why did you join the Navy?
To once and for all, get away from my mother.

Where did they send you?
Great Lakes boot camp in Chicago.

From there where were you stationed?
At a naval air center in Pax [Patuxent] River, Maryland.

What was your job in the Navy?
To pick up pilots who crashed in the ocean. These were mainly test pilots trying out new equipment. From the air center, we would go out with rescue boats and find them.

What was your classification?
I was classified as "fireman." I would work in the engine room.

Does that mean you put out fires?
No, I worked on the engines. The blue stripes were "seaman," they worked above deck. The red stripes were "fireman," they worked below deck. The green stripes were "aviation."

How long were you in the service?

I was in for three years. It was during the Bay of Pigs.$_{24}$ That was when the Russians were trying to bring in missiles to Cuba.$_{25}$ We stopped them at the three mile limit. We told them if they crossed that limit, we would blow them right out of the water. Our particular people were on submarine watch. We would drive around on a sound boat. We would have different sonars and radars that would pick up different sounds from the Russian submarines. That was before they had what we now call, "Silent Submarines." We were doing sub duty, so they couldn't sneak in at the three mile limit.

Since we're talking around that time era, who do you think killed Kennedy?

I believe Johnson had something to do with it. The assassination$_{26}$ happened in Texas and Johnson was from Texas. The organized crime people had Ruby kill Oswald because Ruby was dying of cancer anyway.

When did you leave the Navy?

It was 1963. They first tried to give me a medical discharge. I believe it was for my hearing. When I refused it, they gave me a discharge which read, "Honorably discharged for the convenience of the government." But then I lost my DD214 papers.

What's that?

It's my discharge papers. I lost them when my apartment caught fire. For three years I've been trying to get new papers to replace them. There's just no reason it should take that much time. With all the red tape, they just keep putting me off. I can't get any type of benefits without them.

After you left the Navy, what did you do?

I went back to work at the racetracks.

How long has it been since you quit working at the tracks?
About 12 years ago.

Did you have any other jobs?
I worked for an automotive company for 11 years, but I got hurt on the job. I slipped on the oily floor and hurt my back. I collected 85% of my pay until it was time to go back. They finally settled on $250,000 and I quit.

What happened to that money?
The government took it away for back child support.

How long were you married?
About two years. I had a little girl. The last time I saw her was when she was 12 years old.

What was the reason for your divorce?
I lost my mother and daughter within nine days of each other.

I don't understand. I thought your daughter was still alive?
I had two daughters. The one that died was nine days old. She only weighed two pounds. I blamed my wife for the baby's death.

Can you explain?
She didn't do anything the doctors told her to do. She would do anything she damn well pleased. When you're pregnant, you don't go for walks on the icy streets in the middle of night.

Did she fall?
I'm not sure, but the baby was born premature because of it. (I must have missed something, but I did not pursue it)

Did you get any pensions from your past jobs?
No, all I get is about $800 a month from Social Security. In fact, when I first started getting it, the amount was around $600.

So, how did you get to where you are today?
I had a fire in my apartment. It was government subsidized.

Why didn't you just get another apartment?
The woman who was in charge said, "I will guarantee that you will never get another subsidized apartment again." She said I started the fire on purpose.

What happened?
I went to blow out a candle and my oxygen started the fire.

You weren't smoking?
No, when I went to blow the candle out, I forgot the oxygen was on. My apartment was the only one destroyed. At first, it was just a little fire. I went and grabbed the fire extinguisher, but this guy showed up and pulled it out of my hands. I guess he thought it would be better by attacking the fire from the outside. If I could find that guy today, I think I would hurt him. He's the one who caused the big problem. I could have put it out in a matter of seconds.

After your apartment caught fire, where did you go?
I have no family and at that time my Crohn's[27] disease was acting up, so they put me in the hospital. After that, I was transferred to a low-end rehab place like the one I'm at today. They have transferred me to several places. I've been trying to get out of the system for three years.

Why did they move you from the last place you were at?
They conveniently kept running out of my medication, and the little money I had ended up missing. So I told them, "The hell if I'm going to pay any money to stay here." So, they moved me to this hole where I'm at today.

Since this place is state subsidized, how would you compare it to the last rehab you were in?
This place has no efficiency at all. I have been here eight weeks and have yet to see a doctor.

Who prescribes your medicine?
I have no idea.

What do they give you?
I know they give me Doxepin[28] for anxiety and Oxycodone[29] for pain. All the other stuff, I have no idea.

Where is your pain?
I have it in my neck and back.

Was that from your accident at the automotive company?
No, not at all. Three of my biker friends and I were hit by a drunk driver. The driver killed two and crippled two. I was all broke up. I was in the hospital four months.

Did you get any money for that?
By the time I got out of the hospital, there was no money left from the settlement.

Did veterans take care of you in the hospital?
No, not at all.

Why not?
Because I don't have the DD214 papers.

Shouldn't they be easy to get?
The place I was in before tried to help me, but they also had no success. I gave them my Social Security number and my service number, but that didn't help either.

When it's time to leave here, where will you go?
That's my problem. I have no family and no one will take me anywhere to find an apartment.

I have two questions. Can you live on $800 a month and are you stable enough to live alone?
I lived by myself before my apartment caught fire. I can find a place for $600 a month. That leaves me $200 for whatever. Plus, I can get food stamps.

Don't they have a case worker in this place to help you?
They are supposed to, but I haven't seen anyone for that either. All I need is for someone to take me out of here and get me a newspaper. I will find an apartment.

Can you get around?
If I stand up, it is hard for me to see because my back is bowed over so far, I'm mainly looking down at the floor. If I sit in my cart, I can see fine.

So, let me get this straight. You've been homeless for three years going in and out of rehabs?
That's right. And like I said, I'm in no different shape now then I was three years ago.

Where do you see your future?
I don't see any future. They expect me to die in here and if they keep feeding me that crap, I will die.

Do you have any money saved?
Yeah, I have about two grand stashed.

Do you mean in the bank?
No, I have it stashed where no one can find it.

Do you spend any of your money while you're here?
You better believe I do. If I eat this shit food day after day, I'll get sick.
I usually order pizza or some other type of carryout.

If you get an apartment, how would you get furniture?
I have friends in the motorcycle club. They're called "The Penetrators."

What are the Penetrators like?
We are our own club. We never cause problems. We like to help people.
You got a few good apples and a few bad apples in every club, but for
the most part we're good. You would be really surprised how much
money the Penetrators have donated to charity.

Do you have a driver's license?
No, they took it away. I was just on my way back from my brother's
funeral in Chicago when I got a flat tire. The cop shined his flashlight in
my eyes and said, "Your eyes are pinned." Hell, your eyes would be
pinned too if someone was shining a light in your eyes.

You weren't drinking or on drugs?
I don't drink and the only drugs I take are what a doctor gives me. And
besides, I forgot to take my medication on that trip.

**If you weren't drinking and you weren't on drugs, why did they
take your license?**
When they checked my license they said it was suspended. I told the
cop, "I never got a ticket before. Why am I suspended?" He told me
that he didn't know, but then I found out that I forgot to renew it on
my birthday.

**Since you're in a rehab/nursing home, what rehab do they put you
through?**
Not a damn thing. And besides, what's there to rehab? There's nothing
they can do about my neck or back.

What about your Crohn's? Can they do anything for that?
Over the years, I've had five operations. When I eat something, it still goes right through me. It's because they have taken out so much small and large intestines.

Is there anything else you would like to say?
Just that I would like to get a copy of my discharge papers. That way the military could help me.

After leaving, I had this urge to help him get a copy of his discharge papers. The next day I started calling places from American Legions to VA hospitals. I didn't know exactly where to call, but the research continued for days. Recently my father, who is a WWII veteran, gave me a phone number from one of his letters from the VA. Hopefully, this will lead me in the right direction. Here I am with a cell phone and a number to call that might lead to finding his papers, but it's still not an easy task. I can only imagine how hard it is for a 72 year old man lying in bed all day with no one to help him.

The Oldest Profession

At this point, I thought that there was just about enough material for my book. Then I remembered a girl who was panhandling about a mile up the expressway from my first interview. She was Caucasian, had long black hair, and was sitting on a bucket. There were two things about her that stuck in my mind. Number one, she had a very "stone-like" look on her face. Two, I remember watching as she got into a car after a man handed her some money. At the time I had a feeling of what she was up to by the way she was dressed, but I didn't have enough guts to approach her. It would have been my first interview, and I just wasn't ready for that type of hard core story. Now with 17 interviews under my belt, I felt more comfortable approaching her. If she was prostituting, I didn't want to scare her off, since she might think I was a cop. On the other hand, I didn't want to get arrested for picking up a prostitute. So, I was determined to try and interview her on the street. The last thing I wanted was to have her get into my car.

It was Wednesday afternoon on a warm summer day when I exited the expressway and there she was, provocatively dressed, standing next to an old five-gallon plastic bucket. After parking my car on a side street about a block away, I walked up to her with my normal smile. She looked at me, but did not return it. Introducing myself, we shook hands and exchanged names. After giving her a full explanation of why I was there, I asked if she would be willing to tell me her story. I brought along a copy of the front cover of my book, feeling that this would add credibility to the interview. She asked me if I was some type of undercover cop. I assured her that the reason for my visit was solely for the purpose of the book. Finally, after convincing her that everything was on the up and up, we walked over to a nearby wooden bench that was located next to an old abandoned hardware store. We both got comfortable and the interview started.

How old are you?
I'm 33.

What nationality are you?
German and American Indian.

Were you raised in any religion?
Not really.

Do you follow any religion now?
I believe in God.

Are your parents married?
They were never married. My father was in a bar band and that's where they both met. My parents lived together for two years and then I was born.

Are they still together?
No, my father was drunk one day and rolled his car over into a ravine. He lived for a couple days, but then died.

How old were you at that time?
I was 14.

Do you have any siblings?
No.

How far did you get in school?
I quit after the 10th grade.

Why didn't you finish school?
I had no drive to continue.

Was there any abuse in your family?
I would rather not talk about it.

Can I just ask you if it was verbal or physical?
It was a little of both. (Getting answers was like pulling teeth.)

Was it your mother or father that abused you?
It was my dad's brother.

So, you mean your uncle?
Since I had no respect for him, I never used the word uncle.

Where is he at today?
Thank God he's dead.

How did he die?
Cancer.

It would really help me understand your story a little better if you told that part of your life. Would you like to try?
Don't get me wrong. It's not that. I want to tell you what happened, but I'm just not sure where this is all going.

Like I told you at the beginning, no one will know who you are. There will be no names or addresses. But if you feel uncomfortable, let's just skip it. So when did you leave home?

I left right after school was out when I turned 15. I really do want to tell you what happened. It's not that I haven't told other people. It's because I just met you.

Everything you tell me is your choice. Would you like me to ask a different question, or do you want to talk about what happened with your dad's brother?

I will tell you, only because I trust you. My father had a band with two other guys and his brother. They would get together once a week and practice in the garage. As usual the women would sit with them as they all drank and got high. At the end of every practice, everyone would leave except my dad's brother. The first time it happened was one week after my 13th birthday. I remember it was a very hot summer night. We could never afford air conditioning and I was having a hard time falling asleep. It was around three in the morning when this bastard decided to come into my room. He asked me to touch him, but I refused. So, he took my hand and put it on his pants right over his penis. I went to scream and he put his other hand over my mouth. He told me if I made a noise, he would make sure that my mother and father would never see me again. At 13 years old, I believed everything he said. That's all that happened the first time. The following weekend he came into my room and it happened again, but this time he dropped his pants. As the weeks went on, it got worse and worse. At first I didn't understand some of the things he would ask me do, but I went along with everything he said. Then at the age of 14 it was all over. Come to find out my father and him got in a big fight and he ended up getting kicked out of the band. I didn't see him much after that. I decided to leave the house around 10 months later.

Where did you go?

I went to live with my aunt. I wasn't getting along at home with my mother, so I just left. My mother let me go because she figured I wouldn't be gone long, but she was wrong.

You said your father died when you were 14. Was it before or after you left?

It was six months before I left.

At any time, didn't you want to live back at home?

Not really. I blamed my mother and father for what happened.

Don't you now realize that it wasn't your parents' fault?

Oh yeah it was. If there was no drinking or drugs in the house, it probably wouldn't have happened.

How long did you live with your aunt?

For about a year. Then I met this boy who was two years older than me. At first things were good, but then I started freaking out.

What happened?

It really wasn't his fault. As time went on we started fooling around. But every time he wanted me to do something sexually, he would use the same words that my dad's brother would use. We finally broke up and I ran away from my aunt's house.

Where did you go from there?

I had this friend from high school. My mother didn't like me hanging around her because she used drugs. She lived with her drug dealer boyfriend. I told her I had no place to live, so they took me in.

How did that go?

There was very little quiet time. People were in and out all hours of the night. He was mainly selling heroin. I never saw him use it, but my girlfriend was shooting up several times a day. Many times she would ask me if I would try it, but at that time it scared me to death. As time went on we became a threesome. Not sexually, but we were inseparable as friends.

Did you help sell the drugs?
Not exactly, but my friend and I made people feel comfortable when they showed up.

Are you on heroin now?
Sad to say I am.

How did that start?
About 10 years ago, I was at a low in my life. Things were going nowhere. I was self-medicating with pills and it was getting pretty bad. One night I finally gave in to my girlfriend. When she shot me up for the first time, it seemed that all my troubles went away. At first I really tried to limit myself, but that didn't last long.

How much do you use today?
A lot. It's a morning, noon, and night.

Are you homeless now?
I guess you can say I am. I live about two blocks from here with eight other people. It's just a place to stay at night.

What happened to your two close friends?
I'd rather not say.

Why don't you want to talk about it?
Just in case they read your book one day.

Ok, let's change the subject. What does your sign say?
It reads, "Will work for food. Homeless."

When I first noticed you, I saw you get in a car. Then when I drove by another time you were getting in another car. Do you want to tell me what that's all about?
I'm sure you can figure it out.

How long have you been doing that?
It's been about 10 years now.

How did you get started?
When I started panhandling, I was making $30 to $50 a day and one of my friends was making a couple hundred dollars a day. I knew what she was doing and with the cost of my habit rising, I made a decision to try it.

What was it like the first time?
There was this man around 60 years old. He stopped and handed me $20. We started some small talk and I asked him if he was lonely. The next thing I knew is that we were in the car together looking for a vacant alley. We agreed on oral sex and I made him put on a condom. To this day, if they don't want to use a condom, then the deal's off.

But didn't you feel pretty low the first time?
Remember, I started at an early age.

How many tricks do you pull a week and what do you charge?
Friday is usually my best day. I may do five or six in a 24 hour period. I charge whatever the situation will bring.

Like how much?
I'd rather not say.

Do you have any STDs?
I'm clean. I've always stuck to my condom policy.

Has anything bad ever happened to you on the streets?
Yeah, this one time I was picked up by this guy who looked a little odd. He reminded me of a man who couldn't get a woman because he was so ugly. I know that sounds bad, but it is what it is. Anyway, after I got in his car he asked if I would like to go to his place. Feeling a little nervous, I had this gut notion something was wrong. Every time he would talk to me there was no eye contact and he would always repeat himself. We finally got a room in one of those by the hour places. The room had a mirror over the bed and the toilet seat was busted. The man asked me to take off my clothes and lay on the bed. When I asked him to join me, he started to take off his belt. Once he removed it, there was this cold look that came over his face. Before I knew what was going on, he started whipping me. The worst part was that he was hitting me with the buckle end. See this scar on my leg? I took seven stitches where he hit me. As he was beating me, I hauled off and kicked him as hard as I could right in the balls. As he fell to the ground, I shot out of the door. Running around with no clothes on, I was picked up by the cops.

Did they catch the guy?
Hell no! Do you think the cops are going to help someone like me? They see this stuff all the time in Detroit.

What did you learn from that experience?
I now try to memorize their license plate before I get in their car. I also carry some protection.

What kind of protection?
Let's just say I feel a lot safer now.

Do you want to quit what you're doing?
Sure I do, but don't know how. If you have the answer, please let me know.

Do you have any children?
Nope.

Do you want children?
Hell no. They'll probably end up just like me.

Is there anyone you can trust to get help?
About two years ago I met this guy at a party. We went out a couple times. I'm one who believes in telling the truth, so I told him about my life style. I never saw him again. I feel he was the type of person that could have been trusted.

At the rate you're going, how long do you think you'll live?
Who cares, I was handed a bad deal and now I have to live with it till the end.

I think your story will help a lot of people who were sexually abused at a young age. What do you think?
If my story just helps just one person, then I'm glad it's been told. I should of got help, but didn't know better.

One last question before I leave. If you could change your life, how would you want it to be?
I don't fantasize. I just play life day by day. This is my world and I'm going to stick to it.

After finishing the interview, I have come to the conclusion that each and every street person has their own individual story. It is difficult to evaluate and understand their situation until the whole story is told, and hard to comprehend without actually being in their shoes.

A Subliminal Life

"A man who lives everywhere, lives nowhere."
Marcus Valerius Martialis [Roman poet 86-AD]

Pulling out of my subdivision, heading for work one day, I noticed what appeared to be a homeless man standing on the side of the road. Although all the interviews had been completed, I had this overwhelming impulse to do just one more. Pulling the car over, I crossed the street and introduced myself. I asked if he was homeless, "No I am not," he replied. The man explained that his pup tent was with him at all times as he traveled throughout the United States. I gave him my pitch, requested an interview and he agreed. After asking why he was on the road, the guy explained that it was to spread his message across the nation. I asked with the utmost curiosity, "What message is that?" That's when things started going haywire.

He started to explain, but I had no idea what he was talking about. I told him to hold on a minute and tried to make it clear that his story needed to be told in such a way that readers could understand. The man was obviously intelligent, but his mental state seemed questionable. I decided to forge ahead with the interview anyway. His answers may be hard to comprehend at times. In fact, some of them may make no sense at all, but they are written word for word just as they were recorded. In addition, resources for some of the organizations mentioned could not be verified.

May I ask your age?
I'm 63. I was born in 1953.

Are your parents still alive?
As far as I know, my mother is.

How long were your parents married?
They were married 15 years before they ended up getting divorced.

Did they bring you up in any religion?
My mother was a devout Catholic and my father was nothing. One thing they both agreed on was to let us children choose our own religion.

So, what did you choose?
Nothing.

How old were you when they got divorced?
I was 15.

How did you handle that?
It was okay. My mother was very loving, but he was heavy handed. My parents owned their own restaurant, so things seemed pretty good. Where the problem came in was when my father took up with one of the waitresses. My whole family knew about it. My mother had to work side by side with her. So when they got divorced, my parents just went their own ways.

Were you abused as a child?
I believe I ended up with what's called "baby shaking syndrome."[30] From the age four to six my father shook me to stop my crying. I remember making the conscious decision that I was observing something that I needed to pay attention to.

How far did you get in school?
Eleventh grade, I was a high school dropout. In 1981, I did receive a GED.

Do you have any substance abuse?
In my younger years I drank a lot of beer and smoked a lot of pot, but at that time I considered it a novelty.

Tell me about your siblings.
I had six brothers and four sisters. I was right in the middle. They are all doing very well.

Do you keep in touch with them?
No, because I attempted a suicide in the year 1996.

How did you attempt it?
I shot myself in the chest with a nail gun. I'm a carpenter by trade. I normally don't carry a knife or a firearm.

Why did you do that?
Because I had been victimized by a high ranking government official. I realized how severely they had me hamstrung.

Who was this government official?
I'd rather not say.

Please explain what happened.
I was in a relationship and poised to be married for the first time in 1995. I was also starting my own business in residential repair. As I was working, the residents that I were doing repairs for suddenly turned their back on me. Consequently, what I learned was that the government official had forfeited me to a rolling craps game process, which he and his family routinely prospered by way of. I was just a puppet in the system.

Can you break it down as to why you tried to kill yourself?
It was in response to organized crime abuse. My response was very deliberate. When I was done working that day, I checked myself into a hotel room and that's where I did the deed.

Did you call anyone?
I called up my fiancé and told her if she didn't fess up to me, then I had no reason to live.

Fess up about what?

I had the sneaking suspicion that I had been financially defrauded while I was with her. What I learned since is that she was a relative of the official. It was he and his shitheads that were financially defrauding me. Since my fiancé was the only one in my life, everything happened through her discrete communication with this guy's cronies. I was genuinely surprised, after living with her for two years, that this was going on. At the time, she and I were going to endeavor in real estate speculation.

When you shot yourself, where were you, and who found you?

I was in a hotel and I'm not sure who found me. I just woke up in a hospital. You're not going to believe this one. I was always told my heart was on the left side. So when I shot myself, I missed my heart and blew out a lung. At that point they offered me SSI assistance, but I refused it. Instead I decided to forsake any mental health assistance and more importantly go after the seat of organized crime that had been financially defrauding me. So in a sense, in regards to the National Course Correcting Coalition that I'm associated with now, the financial defrauding I had suspected has since been confirmed by investigators, and they know specifically the people who were involved.

But, don't you think the organized crime people just let you continue your story because they feel you hold no credibility?

I do precisely. And your assessment is correct in that a group of sociologists and psychiatrists were recommending that very idea when things began. What they told the senior congressional representatives was that if you allow the seat of organized crime to continue to persecute, once they lock horns, they won't yield in such regards. And here is the significance of these parallel lines of thought. When the discussions began eight years ago, regarding National Course Correction, fewer than 100 people of organized crime in our nation could be identified by the senior congressional representatives. Once they started persecuting me, they would not relent. Today there are over 50,000 identified in organized crime. So in a sense, the legitimate house within American Government took advantage of the persecution that he and others who affected me personally, and used as much to specifically identify just whom the seat of organized crime is in our nation. So, I do not begrudge their taking advantage of me in such regards.

Let me give you a synopsis of what most people misunderstand about the United States of America. I mentioned earlier for the National Course Correction to even have a snow ball's chance in heck, we had to win the support of the grand old GOP.[31] The correlation herein being a group known as Klan Destin Intelligence imbedded within the GOP. They actually have been developing over 160 years. This is how far back the Klan Destin unit has been with the GOP. They started to embellish their group into war time racketeering and profiteering. So over the years of wars, the council has profited to its advantage. These councils that we have retrospectively numbered, is mostly remembered for the Ninth Council. It started eight years before World War II and went on till 1962. What this group represented was unprecedented and unparalleled. This group had been traditionally a Klan Destin Intelligence unit within the GOP. For the first time ever they established themselves as a regime.

At that time, they were free to micromanage the American Government. Life in the United States of America actually got turned upside down overnight in the early 1960's. Eisenhower[32] was fully aware that the Ninth Counsel was the seat of organized crime. He was intending to undermine them. So, Eisenhower picked John F. Kennedy as the succeeding president. They were on the same page knowing where the origin of problems in our nation was originating from. In other words, they both knew that the Ninth Counsel was corrupt.

Where are you going with all of this?

Here's the surprise. A third party entered the situation. The third party stemmed from unresolved World War II issues. Along came Himmler[33] from the Third Reich, under Hitler.[34] The counsels were not affiliated to the American lineage alone. It was always international. Himmler had greater communications in technology than Eisenhower and John F. Kennedy had perceived. This caused a couple of ramifications that occurred. The Vietnam War[35] was initially started by Eisenhower because he was trying to draw out the war time profiteers. By doing this, he could bring the war time profiteers in the open. At that point his plan was to stop the war and close out the Ninth Counsel, but Eisenhower was blindsided and not able to end the war because of this character named Hitler. Here is the significance of Hitler's participation. A man by the name of Nellis[36] was a council ideologist and as well the head of the United States Air Force. Himmler was a crony of the original commander, Nellis. From the close of World War II forward, Himmler actually relocated to the United States of America. Nellis provided him sanctuary. [The Vietnam War started on November 1, 1955, long after Hitler was gone. U.S. involvement was limited until March 8, 1965 when the first American combat troops waded ashore at China Beach north of Da Nang. In addition, history shows that Himmler committed suicide on May, 23 1945 while in British custody.]

Can you please explain?

In short, Kennedy's assassination had no motive other than to show the declaration that Himmler had succeeded. So, Nellis helped supply resource limited Germany to a position in the United States of America with all of the resources the U.S. had to offer.

Let's get back to your life. Where do you live now?

I have been traveling since 1996.

Why are you traveling?
I am nothing more than a coalition volunteer. When I travel jurisdiction by jurisdiction, this gives the proponents of National Course Correction the opportunity to initiate dialog with city leadership in a dynamic developing continuum.

How do you get your money?
I simply rely on hand outs.

What if no one wants to give you money?
I starve in between. At first, there were 2,500 of us, but now that there are 68,000,000 of us. The money comes much easier.

Do the police ever bother you?
Mostly they avoid me.

Why do you think they avoid you?
Because of the government officials scare stories. They suggest that a visual connect with me would prove hazardous to them. There's nothing to that. Actually, it works the exact opposite. The discussions within me are 24 hours a day.

What do you mean by the discussions within you?
We can get to that in a little bit.

Where do you go to the bathroom?
I tend to eat light. On occasion I use the outdoors as a restroom, but most of the time I do not.

Where do you pitch your tent?
I usually get off the road far enough where the traffic noise will diminish.

What brought you to Michigan?
We have been working a five state coalition of Kentucky, Tennessee, Indiana, Ohio, and Michigan.

How do you keep in touch with everyone?
I support an embedded transceiver.

How did you get this embedded transceiver?
When I attempted suicide, I was subsequently furnished an embedded transceiver.

What exactly is an embedded transceiver?
It's a radio device which was embedded below my left lung. This device transmits and receives radio signals. Thus, explains about the discussions within me.

How do you receive those signals?
Subliminally as well as audibly.

What was the purpose of the doctors putting this device in your body?
Organized crime uses the transceivers in as many people as possible. However, the American Government uses the transceivers on the other end for protection. During the eight years that I said we advanced congress and justices with the specifics of who constituted the seat of organized crime, it went from fewer than 100 to over 50,000 people. What we also learned is that today there are over 46,000,000 of these devices embedded in U.S. citizens that were not disclosed to the American Government.

Do all the people who have these transceivers in their body know they have them?
Not necessarily.

Can organized crime or the government track you with this device?

Yes, but not only that, it's a way the communication people better understand the full potential of the receiver's capability. They wanted me specifically outfitted with one, as a test case.

So, you were the first case?

No, there were three other cases that failed since 1960.

Why did they pick you?

Because I was being touted by some people in the intelligence community as someone who could get the job done in terms of identifying the seat of organized crime within our nation. I do not begrudge the people who conspired against me when they outfitted me with the transceiver because their objectives are generally known. Constitutional government for all proposes is derailed. Therefore, the citizens have to resurrect the constitutional government. Do you recognize the correlation between what was happening with Abraham Lincoln[37] and what is going on now? Even Mr. Lincoln had to deal with it back then. He was concerned that a government that was established of the people, by the people, and for the people, might perish from the earth. The same shitheads are doing the same shit that they got away with back then. He identified a festering problem that has not gone away even today.

These subliminal messages that you receive, what do they consist of?

I get subliminal messages from the seat of organized crime as well as well as from the legitimate house of American Government.

Can each organization pick up what the other one is sending?

Yes, this was the whole reason for "The Legitimates" conspiring to get me hard wired with the transceiver.

Am I to understand that you keep hearing messages back and forth between the good and the bad?
Yes, and I'm caught in the middle.

Doesn't that drive you crazy?
(Maybe I shouldn't have worded it that way.) I get genuine feedback in regards to the progress we're making in terms of the coalition's efforts. They encourage my sane and continued participations by virtue of educations as well as moral support.

The next question I'm going to ask you, I don't mean to sound condescending, but I'm going to just come out with it. What do you say to the people who think that you're psychotic, and that you think there is a device planted within your abdomen?
It's not my role to convince anyone of anything. As I stated, my principle role is to provide the computer firms amalgam with the mobile and benign focal points that they require for the analysis of the primary communication system, which is corrupted. Not at any time did they say that I would have to convince the people that I cross paths with.

When was this device planted inside you?
In 1996, when my lung had collapsed from the attempted suicide. They simply spread open my rib cage on my left side and slipped in the device.

You seem intelligent enough to for me to ask this next question. Is there a possibility that this is all just made up in your mind?
I don't believe so. What you're getting at is what we call self-serving logic. Not in the least do I believe this is not real. As I said earlier, the decisions in my head go on 24 hours a day. The only time I'm not listening is when I'm sleeping. Let me explain how I rationalize this. I hear from some of the most intelligent people our nation has to offer. I hear consistently from the seat of organized crime, trying to justify their actions. I've heard feedback from the communications people that one

of the reasons that law enforcement are responding as distantly as they are at this point and time is that the communications people have in effect given up on pressing the visual connect. They can simply initiate their dialog with the law enforcement that happened to pass by in near vicinity to my transceiver.

How would this receiver still be working to this day without any recharge?
AM radio relies on the manipulation of the ionosphere.[38] Also, organized crime has embedded transceivers in most TVs so they can keep an eye on people like you in their own household. They refer to those as the desk top appliance transceivers.

Do you believe that aliens control any of this?
Not in the least.

Have you ever met anyone else with one of these devises?
I do daily. Remember, there are 46,000,000 embedded in US citizens.

I had my appendix removed three years ago. Are you telling me I might have one of these devices in me?
Yes, let me explain. When I was convalescing after my operation, I was feeling sensations that were completely new to me. At that point, I started questioning what was going on. The feeling had nothing to do with the trauma that I went through. One of the things that I was mulling over, while lying in the hospital room, was that whoever initiated the Oklahoma City bombing[39] may have had a hand in undermining my life. So from 1996 forward, I actually made four separate trips to Oklahoma to talk with the victims' families. I was wondering if there was any coloration between what had happened in Oklahoma City and the personal victimization of what happened in my life. What I have learned since, from the proponents of National Course Correction, is that the high level official is one of the correlations. Years later I was advised that there actually was a connection.

Am I to understand that both the good and the bad can make you do things by contacting you through subliminal messages?

Yes, you are beginning to see the light with regards to state of the art virtual communications. A lot of the communication was developed by Hitler during his experimentation on the Jews. Many times when people get migraine headaches, it can be triggered by a communications fling. The Germans are the ones mainly responsible for cancer flinging in general. In other words they keep the population in check. The people who have developed this are called pecking order ideologists. They are basically the seat of organized crime.

The people who don't have the radio device in them, how do they acquire cancer?

It is introduced into the food chain by the people in organized crime. It works as the same process as crystal radio. A crystal radio can simply be made from a toilet paper roll and some strips of copper or aluminum. The only thing that you need to extract audio voices from the air is a crystal diode that can be purchased at any hardware store. The making of a crystal diode which can develop in our personal system is known as MSG. [Monosodium Glutamate – a food additive] If people consume enough MSG, their brain becomes a platform for crystal radio technology.

Why do they want these cancers in people?

Because when this started the Germans wanted control of the pecking order, and develop the master race. They wanted to dominate everyone they could. The development of this radio system was a platform for a weaponry system.

What is your mission from here?

You have to understand, my fiancé and I were setting things up for retirement. We wanted to purchase old homes and rebuild them for sale. We ended up both being fleeced. We were not allowed to succeed.

Why didn't the high government official want you to marry into the family?

Because, she is known as the membership. I was never the membership. Some people felt that I may discuss a platform for National Course Correction.

So again, where are you going from here?

I have been denied gainful employment from 1996 forward. It is the government that stops me from getting a job. There is a transcript in which the official indicates that I will not be allowed to earn one dollar. This is because I am accused of not paying on unpaid taxes. This is one of the tools the seat of organized crime uses to disparage me. They denied me gainful employment, so I can't pay my taxes. There is a robotic sustenance which also is used to control our actions. Temporary insanity is an explanation for the controlling devices used by organized crime. Again, all I want to do is resume gainful employment.

That's not going to happen. You understand why, don't you?

I assume you mean the determination for employment would be based on my suicide. I'm not intending to prosper by virtue of assisting the senior congressional representatives with their obligation to resurrect the constructional government.

But, don't you understand that a company will not keep you on the job site because of your views on what we talked about?

You may be correct, but there are many other pitfalls that we haven't discussed that would also stop me from gainful employment. Until we get our governmental house in order, we are all victims of double standards. I guess I will just continue what I'm doing until the law enforcement will climb on board. Eventually, we as a nation will have to replace the corruptible audio system with a new and securable communication system which is being developed. We need people to stop using their heads for just hat racks and start thinking more sensibly.

Is there one last thing you would like to say?
Everything that has been discussed in terms of National Course Correction will at some point be revealed in American history.

With the last interview under my belt, I realized that no matter how good things are, any situation can change for the worse. Anyone can get caught up with drugs, crime or poverty. It may not happen directly, but it sure could happen indirectly. It could happen just from being in the wrong place at the wrong time. I had to find out for myself. It was time to go out and panhandle, so that I could experience firsthand how the homeless survive. In my mind, I tried to make excuses for not going, but for every excuse that told me no, there were 10 reasons that told me yes. What I was about to do was way out of my comfort zone, but I looked at it like this - there are no guarantees in life.

It's My Turn

The first thing I had to do was make a sign. From my observations, all signs were made from cardboard and most of them were so beat up that they were almost unreadable. Below is a list of a few signs that I encountered.

1: Will work for food

2: Homeless, need work

3: Just a smile is good enough

4: Veteran, need help

5: I don't have to lie, need money for a beer

6: Out of work, wife, and children, homeless

7: Homeless, I do not use drugs

8: Will do anything for money

9: Just lost job, don't ask me why

10: Help the homeless, will come back tenfold

Since I was not homeless, I didn't want the sign to be a lie. So, I decided that it would simply say, "Help the Homeless, God Bless." Additionally, I made a conscious decision early on that when people gave me money, I would hand them a typed letter explaining exactly what I was doing. See copy of the letter below:

Are you being scammed?

When you give your hard earned money to the panhandlers on the street, are you being scammed?

I am not homeless. All of the money I collect on the street today will be donated to Gleaners Food Bank.

My name is Terry Celano and I am nearly at the completion of my Book, *One Leg and a Cup*.

This very intriguing book tells true, up close and personal stories of people who live on the streets. They tell their stories from childhood up to present time and all of the hard times in between. Each person's interview was recorded and their conversations in my book are relayed word for word.

Each person was paid for their story and at no time do I release their names or specific locations.

WARNING

Because of the raw and blunt nature of the actual stories provided, this book may not be sutable for all readers.

As I previoulsy stated, I am near the end of my book. My experience panhandling on the streets will be told in my last chapter to bring *One Leg and a Cup* to it's conclusion.

To Pre-Order your book today, please go to www.onelegandacup.com

There is a discussion section on my website and I would love to hear from you. All comments are welcome.

Thank you for your time.

Terry Celano

..

Next, I needed to find some old clothes that would fit the part I was about to play. I was once told by a homeless person that panhandlers who dress in dirty-old clothes were the ones who least needed the money. They try to look worse than they really are. I was contemplating a compromise when I remembered that I had some large black plastic bags in the garage that were full of old coats, gloves, and hats. In one of them I found a heavy down-filled coat with an attached hood. I then grabbed a fur lined hat with pull down ear covers. Next, there was a pair of neoprene gloves which are the same type that are used on crab boats. I then found some heavy boots that were good up to 35°F below zero. Finally, I picked out an old bright yellow shirt and a pair of worn out jeans. To further look the part, I decided not to shave for a couple of days before going out.

Later, once out on the street, I realized that the coat originally cost $275; the boots were $125; the shirt was $99 and the gloves, hat, and jeans cost a total of $145. The whole outfit came to a grand total of $644. It wasn't exactly the apparel you would see a homeless person wear, but the clothes looked old and they would keep me warm.

Author ready to panhandle

As I was getting everything ready, a crazy idea popped into my head. "What if I got drunk before going out?" That would not only put me in a state of liquid courage, but it would also give me the appearance of a panhandler with that blank look on his or her face that I saw so often. Pondering that thought for a while, I finally decided against it for three reasons: I didn't want to get arrested for public intoxication; being drunk on a busy corner didn't sound very safe; a bad hangover didn't seem appealing.

I didn't want to panhandle too close to my home town because someone might recognize me. My neighbors might think that I was either trying to scam them or that I was broke. I would probably end up all over Facebook or on the front page of the local paper with the headline, "Local business man tries to scam home town." Additionally, I didn't want to set up in a dangerous area where my life could be on the line. It had to be in a town just outside of the Detroit city limits. This way I would still be close to the where a lot of panhandlers gather. I decided that whatever town I chose, the first step would be to contact the local police and get their approval. This would do two things. It would help me to understand the local laws, and it would provide some protection if required.

I decided to go to the town of Livonia, Michigan. Livonia is located about five miles east of Detroit and borders the affluent towns of Northville to the west, and Novi to the northwest. The reason for choosing Livonia was because I have a longtime friend [Phil] who has a son [John] that is a police officer for the city. I called Phil and explained what I was planning to do and asked him to contact his son about panhandling there. After John talked to his supervisor, Phil called back and told me to go down to the police station and explain what I wanted to do. The officers at the front desk were more than happy to accommodate me and even suggested what corner I should stand on. They also told me that the officers on duty would be notified, and to keep an eye on me. Their cooperation was an enormous help and I can't thank them enough. It shows that officers like those in Livonia do care about the homeless.

Over one year had passed since starting this project and it was the day after New Year's when I finally got up enough courage to go out. Luckily it was 42°F and partly sunny. Please understand that I was not going to stay out overnight or interact with other homeless people. I obtained most of the information I needed from my interviews. My goal was strictly to find out what it was like to panhandle. I decided to stay out from 12:00 p.m. to 4:00 p.m.

At first, it was interesting to watch people that were stopped at the traffic light, looking straight ahead as if they didn't see me. In fact, many cars would move over into the center lane just to get away from the curb where I stood. Concealed behind my sign were the letters that I intended to hand out to the people that gave me money. Each one explained exactly what I was doing and included the address of my website. My friend Lindsey came along to film my experience. I planned to use the video as a trailer for my website, and to post it on YouTube.

The first hour was uneventful to say the least. All I collected was a total of seventy-five cents. I didn't get it. What was I doing wrong? Maybe people suspected or somehow figured out that I wasn't homeless. I didn't think they could see Lindsey because he was off to the side filming from behind some bushes.

But then, just like someone turned on a switch, people started handing me money left and right. First it was a couple of ones, then a five. One elderly man handed me a twenty. I compared the experience to fishing. At first they're not biting, but then they "turn on." While standing there, I tried to make a game out of it. Who would give and who wouldn't? It seemed that the upper and lower classes were giving more than the middle class. I tried to determine the worth of the people by the value of their cars. I'm not sure if it was a true correlation to the amount of donations, but it's all I had to go on.

After a couple hours went by, something interesting happened. An old rusted out pickup truck, with busted springs and a couple of broken lights, stopped at the traffic light. There was a bunch of shabby clothes scattered throughout the bed of the truck. Driving the vehicle was a lady that appeared to be in her twenties, with two small children at her side. She put down the window and told me that she had no money. I asked, "Do you need money?" The lady replied, "I don't understand." I then asked, "What is it you don't understand?" Very confused she said, "Why would a homeless person hand me money?" I told her, "I'm really not homeless. Do you need money?" She still didn't quite understand and said with a high pitched voice, "Are you for real?" With the light about to turn green, I handed her a twenty from my wallet. She thanked me and as she drove off I heard her say, "It's a beautiful day."

A few minutes later a guy that looked like he was in his early thirties stopped at the traffic light. The man put down the window and stated that after returning from Iraq, he was hooked on heroin. With a proud look, he stared me straight in the face and said, "I worked the streets for two years, but I kicked the habit and now I hold a good job." He handed me a five and drove off.

After that, an elderly lady stopped and without putting down her window, gave me the sign of the cross. She gazed at me as if the glass was protecting her from the Devil.

All types of people were starting to acknowledge me. One man handed me a plastic bag that contained some change, chewed gum, used toothpicks, and some old wrappers. I figured that this was his way to get rid of garbage and give a donation at the same time.

Another half-hour went by and the Livonia police pulled up with some urgency. They were told that a man was down along the exit of the expressway. At first I had no idea what they were talking about, but then I realized that someone probably saw my videographer lying in the grass from across the road. I explained to them what was going on and after a hearty laugh, they were on their way.

As time went on, I was enjoying conversations with people whether money exchanged hands or not. To my surprise not one person gave me a hard time. In fact, most were more than happy to talk. Maybe it was the positive vibe I was giving off. If on the other hand, I was stressing out because of trying to collect enough money to survive for the day, the amount of donations may have been different. Although my undertaking was short lived, I did conclude that panhandling is a tough way to earn a living and that it is much easier to work than to beg. Of course, some people might consider panhandling as work, although not in the conventional sense, since it is a form of doing something to make money.

After a total of four hours, I collected $110. That comes to $27.50 an hour or $1,100 based on a 40 hour week or $57,200 a year, tax free. That amounts to over $71,000 a year, before taxes. That's well above the average income. The following week I went to Gleaners food bank and donated the $110 that was collected.

Author giving donation to Gleaners Food Bank

Summary

Doing research for this book was quite an adventure. I learned so much and met many new people in the process. Out of all the people I interviewed, not one of them was unkind or disrespectable. Whether they were on crack, a heroin user, an alcoholic or schizophrenic, it made no difference. Some were apprehensive, but eventually they were all willing to tell their story. I suppose they just wanted others to know how tough it can really be on the streets. At least five of them would not accept the money I was offering. They would say, "Give it to someone who needs it more than I do." A common trait was that most came from broken or dysfunctional families. It just goes to show that a family that stays together and functions together stands a much better chance for a successful life.

Most homeless people do not have any real family. I would guess the reason is because, at one time or another, they burned family members that were close enough to help them. Why would they bite the hand that feeds them? Maybe it is because they were exposed at a young age to rape, drugs, murder, incest, and crime.

Although many of the people that I interviewed only went to the 10th or 11th grade, some had their GED and others had college degrees. The amount of education actually had nothing to do with their situation. Street people have just as many rights as we do, but the problem is that they don't know it. Educated or not, most homeless people have no idea how to get help. I did not run into many people who said, "I want to be an alcoholic." Nor did any say, "I want to shoot this heroin till the day I die." In fact, most said that they were caught up in a vicious cycle that they could not get out of.

They live in old abandoned buildings, in their vehicles, make-shift enclosures made of cardboard, under bridges or they take up residence in empty houses with no electricity or running water. Others just curl up on the streets under blankets or whatever else they have to stay warm. They go to the bathroom behind buildings, bushes, and signs; in garbage cans, and dumpsters. They use baby wipes, rags, towels, and paper; whatever they can find to clean up. Sometimes they go to restaurant bathrooms, gas stations or churches to wash up. There are shelters, but many won't go to them because they say that those places are dirty and full of alcoholics and drug addicts. There does seem to be a class structure amongst them. Isn't that ironic?

Surprisingly, there were those who said they were doing okay and did not want help. They indicated that there was more food than a person could possibly eat. It comes from people that drive by, soup kitchens, and churches. Same goes for clothing, but they did indicate the people that were dressed the worse needed the money the least. As far as money is concerned, $30 to $60 seemed to be the average take per day (panhandling from four to six hours). Some did collect Social Security and some were on disability. There were others that had money in the bank or hidden in a "secret place." Many said that only enough money was needed to support their alcohol or drug habits, indicating that they did not feel normal unless drunk or high. Some drank up to a half-gallon of liquor in a 24 hour period and most of the heroin users shot up three times or more a day. A few said they were willing to work and could function when high, but not for long periods of time because of their addictions. Business people know this, so they won't hire them.

Others I interviewed didn't want to get off the streets for various reasons. Maybe it was because they had gone through rehab programs, knew how hard it was, and didn't want to try again. Maybe it was because this was the only life they knew. Maybe it was because they didn't want to face the unknown. They have withdrawn from what we think of as a "normal" society, succumbing to street life. My guess is that most of them are just waiting for a peaceful end to their life. No more pain or misery; not having to worry about where there next bottle or fix will come from. The only person that was working to get off the street was "Ladyfinger." She did smoke cigarettes every once in a while, but had no debilitating addictions.

A number of homeless people actually had health care from the state, but most have to go to hospital emergency rooms to get treatment. Some go so often that they get little help and are kicked out as fast as they come in. Conditions like high blood pressure, high cholesterol, diabetes, and others are not diagnosed, so they don't get medicine that is desperately needed. Most hospitals won't give them the same treatment as someone with insurance. It was not unusual to find that some had been in mental institutions, but a lot of those facilities are gone now. That's too bad because many still have mental issues with little available treatment.

Most of the interviewees were Christians. Seventeen out of nineteen is a substantial number, and many of them have strong faith. In fact, a lot of them attend church services; sometimes more than once a week. When asked if God had failed them, the overwhelming reply was that they were the ones that failed God. I am not sure why many of them have strong faith, but I would guess when a person is down and out, God is the only one that they can rely on.

None seemed interested or wanted to talk about politics except for the man that was interviewed for "A Subliminal Life." Most did not have a high view or confidence in the government. They thought that the government was, at least partially, responsible for their situation. Those that tried to get help found it difficult if not impossible, whether it was from the State or Federal Governments. Most help came from local churches, soup kitchens, and concerned citizens. Interestingly, many had cell phones that were provided to them by the Federal Government. I never did find out how they charged the batteries.

They frequently help each other out, giving extra food, clothing, and money to others in need. They often stick together in groups for protection and comfort. Others just want to be by themselves and have nothing to do with anyone else. None thought that they had a bright future. In fact, many said that they probably would die on the streets.

One of the hardest situations to understand is the dilemma that many homeless veterans are facing. These people have fought for the very gift of freedom we have today. They gave up years of their lives for us, especially the soldiers who fought in wars. Most of them are eligible for free room and board, but there is so much red tape involved. They just don't know where to begin.

Final Thoughts

When people see panhandlers on the street, they judge. Most do have addictions, but through their stories we learn that each and every one has been handed a raw deal. Many of us would say, "They have a choice." Maybe at some point they did, but the longer they are homeless the harder it is to make a lifestyle change. In fact, the percent of people that get off the streets and end up making a good living is practically zero.

Others say they don't want any help. Although some don't, most panhandlers just can't figure how to get out of their situation. For instance, let's take "The Girl Next Door." Here is a young girl who shoots up many times a day. She shoots up early in the morning and then she goes out and begs. When she gets back to her hotel room, around noon, she shoots up again. After that, it is back out on the street where she begs until dark. Once night rolls around, she goes back to her room and shoots up one last time before going to bed. I tried to imagine how scared she must be to have no one to love and console her. It's just her, the drug dealers, and a needle. Hell, I get scared sometimes just walking out the front door in the morning. She grew up believing that God is no more real than Santa Clause. Her mother told her that she wouldn't help because of the drug addiction. Where is the love? If it was my daughter, I would physically drag her off the street and take her to a crises center.

Over the years, I have had several people tell me that they were scammed by a panhandler. A common pitch is, "Do you have a quarter for some food?" Here is one of my favorites, "Will work for food." The point is that if the truth was told, they probably would not collect much money. There are exceptions. One time I was walking down Bourbon

Street in New Orleans at night and saw a man holding a sign that read, "I don't have to lie to anyone; I need money for a beer." Guess what? He collected more money than any of the other nearby panhandlers. I understand that this was just another ploy, but in this rare case, being honest did pay off. "I need money for beer" seemed to be acceptable, but if the sign had said that he needed money for drugs, the outcome would surely have been different.

I have seen beggars that take their children along just to get that pity donation. Now, that's just plain wrong. What a way to raise a child. One time I was at a rest stop in Ohio when a man came up to me with his young son. The man claimed that they were traveling and someone broke into their car and stole his wallet. Then he asked, "Could I borrow $20 for gas, so I can get home?" I pulled him off to the side, so that his son couldn't hear us, and said to him, "Number one, I know you're just trying to scam me. Number two, you have no intentions of ever paying me back." The last thing I said with a stern voice was, "The thing that really bothers me is that you're dragging your son into a situation that will most likely end up shaping his future." The man didn't say a single word as he took my $20. I didn't judge him for taking my money, but I did judge him for possibly screwing up his son's life.

Some people have told me that they will only give to a person that is crippled. Most likely there is a chance that he or she is on disability, but that's still a judgment call. Others said that they saw the same panhandler begging on different corners. There's a reason for that. If a panhandler always worked the same corner, people that use the same route to commute back and forth each day might realize that they already gave to that person. I had one panhandler tell me that if two people were working the same corner, the fresher face ends up collecting the most money.

Not all panhandlers are desperate, but I would say the majority could use a hand out or some other kind of help. Maybe they just need a little guidance on how to get assistance, housing or medical care. It sounds easy, but without knowledgeable friends or relatives, that kind of help is rarely accessible to them. According to the government, we all have some type of health insurance available to us, but it is not always easy to obtain. Sometimes it takes days or even months to figure out how to get the right type of insurance, and that's if you have a computer or phone to work with. You might say, "Why don't they just use the computer at the local library?" Even if they had a way of getting there, most are probably not educated enough to use a computer?

There were the stories about panhandlers who had expensive cars and houses, but I did not find or interview anyone like that. So, the question is, "How do you determine the good from the bad?" The answer is simple - you don't. If we try to judge every homeless person negatively that we come across, then most likely no one would get help. If it makes a person feel good to give, then they should do it. I've come to the conclusion that when afforded the means and opportunity, I just give.

The "Annual Homeless Assessment Report (AHAR) to congress"[40] is a report that is published by HUD every year on the state of the homeless. According to the last report (2016), there were nearly 550,000 homeless people in the United States. Contrary to what some people believe, there are more Caucasian people that are homeless than African American people. The figures include around 40,000 veterans and 36,000 homeless youth (under 18 years of age). The numbers represent an embarrassing stain on American culture. The goal of HUD is to prevent and end homelessness for families, youth, and children by the year 2020. The numbers have declined slightly over the last decade, but because of the complexity of the problem, it is unlikely that they will meet that goal.

The issue slices deep into American society. According the last figures available from the Centers for Disease Control and Prevention, births to unmarried women were holding steady at 40.7 percent.[41] In addition, with the divorce rate hovering around 40% (divorces/marriages), families end up being broken or dysfunctional.[42]

That is the heart of the problem, plain and simple. Until the family unit starts to mean something again, the homeless issue cannot be totally solved.

Visit the sites below to see how you can help:

https://www.onelegandacup.com/

https://www.justgive.org/donations/help-homeless.jsp

Epilogue

Man Hole Cover-up – After the interview, I visited (D) a few times over the next 16 weeks. He was still in the same dirty nursing home, eating their God awful food. Wanting to know what medications he was taking, I asked him to get a list from the front desk. Come to find out that they had him on a total of nine pills; three different opiates, two types of depression medications, and he mentioned four other pills that were not listed. I asked (D) who was responsible for prescribing his pills and how did they determine exactly what was needed? He had no idea.

Finally, the day came when (D)'s Section 8 housing was available. He called me with such excitement, but was worried about how he was going to detox. I talked to the doctor that was familiar with the case and he indicated that (D) was not addicted. After leaving, I called a friend of mine who is an MD and explained the situation. He told me that if (D) was taking those pills for 16 weeks, he was definitely addicted. As far as the drugs were concerned, it looked like there was not a good detox exit strategy from the home. The doctor gave (D) a month's supply of pills and after that he was on his own.

Eventually (D) was moved to a new apartment with the help of his sister. The place was furnished with what looked like almost new furniture. I helped by supplying him with clothes and other necessities. We kept in touch by phone and every once in a while I would visit him. As time went on, (D) started to drink on weekends. It must have been tough not to drink after being on all those pills for several weeks. (D) ended up with a girlfriend who he knew from high school and it seemed like things were going good except for his weekend binges. But then one day, his phone stopped working. He always made sure to call me at least every other week. At the time of this writing there has still been no contact. I hope the guy is ok.

Over the following months, I would go and see **The Girl Next Door** about every two or three weeks. Sometimes I would just wave and other times I would stop and talk to her. On one such occasion, she had on different clothes than the ones I was used to seeing her wear. Additionally, she didn't look like the same soft innocent girl I had grown accustom to. Her face was a black and blue, and her lower lip was swollen. I asked her what happened. She told me that a couple guys stopped and tried to persuade her to get into their car. The girl then went on to say, when she resisted they beat her up and forced her into the vehicle. Then they drove to the hotel where she lived and robbed her of everything. I wasn't sure if she was telling the truth or not, but I offered to help. She refused and asked me to leave.

I tried to visit her again a few times, but the girl was no longer panhandling. This was odd because she seemed to never miss a day out on the streets. Wanting to find out what happened, I decided to visit the hotel where she lived. Even as a teenager I knew this hotel had a bad reputation. I was a little worried about going because the girl told me that the only ones that lived there were drug dealers, users, and prostitutes.

One afternoon on my day off of work, I headed for the hotel. Not only was the hotel depressing to look at from the outside, but bullet proof glass completely surrounded the dilapidated front lobby. The proprietor greeted me at the turnstile window and asked if he could help. Knowing the girls full name, I inquired if she still lived there. He immediately got irate and asked me to leave. After telling the person that I needed a completion to my story, he said that she got into a bad confrontation with some drugs dealers. I wondered if these were the same guys that robbed her. I asked if he knew where she went. Speaking with a deliberate voice, he said, "Maybe she's dead." Then he turned around and walked away.

Like Father Like Son - Since the father and son were begging in my home town, it was not unusual to see them panhandling almost every day near the same entrance to the expressway. Then one day, they just stopped. Curious to know why, I started asking around and found out that they were involved in something that made the national news. It seemed that a car dealership across from where they were standing offered the father and his boy a job, and for some reason they refused.

Still not getting the full story, I went to visit the manager of the enterprise to hear it right from the horse's mouth. Arriving at the dealership, the manager was notified of my presence and was more than happy to talk. He explained that both the father and son were offered a job starting at $10 an hour. They both refused and said they would rather beg for their money. Subsequently, the manager had a sign made and positioned it next to the road in front of the dealership. The sign basically said that the dealership was offering jobs to panhandlers. The story went viral and was the talk of the town.

Next, the manager told me that the father was peeing into a cup across the street from where one of his salesmen was showing a car to a customer. The local police were called and both the father and son were arrested for drunkenness and belligerence. They ended up spending a couple days in jail for the infractions. After the two were released, the father came back and was continually walking back and forth on the lawn of the dealership, flashing his middle finger towards the front window. The father and son finally left because the town people caught on to what was happening and weren't giving them as much money. I recently heard that they are now begging 10 miles east of town.

There are always two sides to every story. From the interview with the father, I felt that he would have a hard time working due to his neurological problems. The son on the other hand looked to be perfectly capable.

One day, while out on the road, I drove by the corner where the woman interviewed for **Quicksand** had panhandled in the past. Knowing that she had a summer job cutting lawns, I really didn't expect her to be there. Surprised that she was, I stopped to talk. Her appearance hadn't changed much other than her hair was much longer than what I remembered, maybe because she was without her wool knit cap. The woman recalled our interview, but forgot my name saying, "What was your name? I remember it was unusual." To which I responded, "The reason it seemed that way is that it's not a name that is used much anymore."

After mentioning my name again, I asked if she and her husband were still in the same situation. She told me that they were, but things were going to change soon. Continuing with, "Now that our grand-daughter is born, my husband and I decided to go to a Methadone clinic near Lansing to get treatment." I reminded her about telling me that Methadone was out of the question because she and her husband would never be completely clean. She remembered, but then told me that they were just getting too old and it was the only way they could figure out how to handle their situation. She gave me a new phone number and wanted me to contact her when my book was published. I left with a good feeling knowing that they were going to try and get help.

I worked with **The Forgotten Veteran** on and off for over a year. Trying to get his military discharge papers was quite a task. It took several days going back and forth on the phone, but I finally found a way to get a copy. They were mailed directly to the nursing home where he was staying. Once again, this demonstrated how hard it is to get anything done when you're homeless. If there's no one available to put in the time to help, it would be very difficult if not impossible for a homeless person to do it on their own.

I didn't see or talk to the veteran as much after that, but then I received a call from him asking for advice, plus he wanted to see me. Since I was still working every day, it wasn't easy finding the time, but I kept telling myself not to use that for an excuse. It's about an hour drive each way from my house to the nursing home. After finally being able to get there, the veteran showed me his bank statement and mentioned that someone at the front desk opened the envelope. Then he showed me a note that was hand written on a piece of torn paper. It read, "You owe bill of 7,000. If you pay by cashier check, they say you can leave." I made it clear to him that it was a federal offence for anyone to open his mail and second, the letter was not signed. I continued by telling him that it looked like an attempt at extortion.

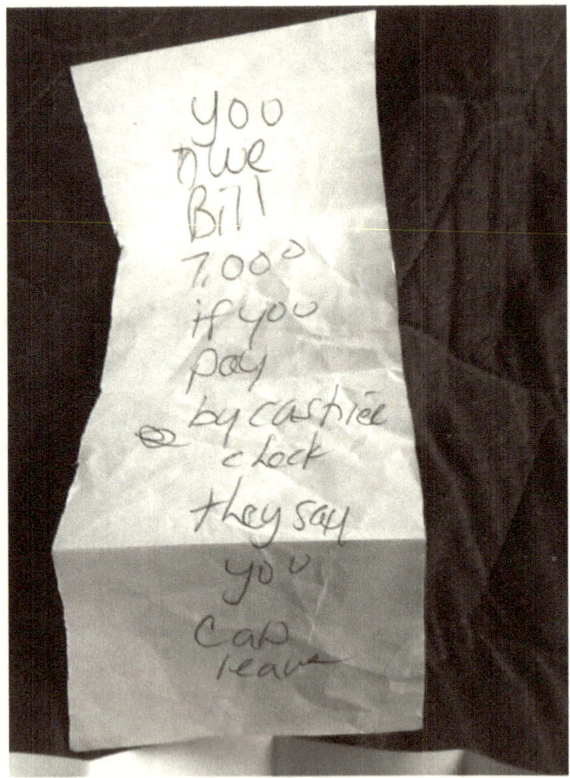

Actual letter

The man reminded me that he had been trying to leave for over a year, but they wouldn't let him out. "Why don't you just get up and go?" I asked. He said that they kept the doors locked at all times and the only way to get out was for them "to buzz you out." I mentioned that was against the law because of the fire code, and that they were holding him against his will.

I wanted to know how much money was in his bank account, thinking that it could be used to help him get a lawyer. He told me that there was around $8,000. I also knew that he received approximately $800 a month in social security benefits. During my original interview, a bank account was not mentioned, saying instead that he had $2,000 stashed where no one could find it. I inquired as to whether he still had that money and he indicated that it was stolen. He went on to say that one night after finishing dinner he became dizzy and passed out. After waking up in the hospital the next morning, they told him that he had a seizure. Apparently he kept the money in his pocket and believing that he was drugged said, "Not only was my $2,000 gone, but they stole a ring right off of my finger."

The next day I contacted two different attorneys and told them about the veteran that needed legal help to get out of a state subsidized home. I also mentioned that he had $8,000 to pay for attorney fees. Neither one of them was cooperative; basically indicating that it was not enough. I pleaded with both of them, "Can't you help a veteran?" It was like asking someone to jump off a bridge. Next I called the Veterans Administration. Actually, it was easier speaking to the lawyers then getting through to anyone there that would help. After calling eight different numbers, the administration referrals came to a dead end. To reiterate, if it was not possible for me to get anywhere, a homeless person surely would not stand a chance.

Months went by and I was getting nowhere. Then I received another call from the veteran. He basically told me that the nursing home was taking him to court, not only for the money that they say he owed, but also to take away his rights. I instructed him to request a court appointed attorney. He should explain that the state subsidized home was holding him against his will and there was possible extortion involved. I also thought it would be best to have him call the police and make a report, so it could be used in court. The court date was set for a Monday about a month later. The veteran asked me to go with him, but I couldn't because a client was coming in from out of state. After the hearing, he called and said that the nursing home attorneys never showed up in court. The judge threw out the case and he had up to 30 days to leave. It made me wonder, "What happens after 30 days?"

My next step was to figure out where he could go. In our phone conversation, the veteran mentioned that he had a sister who lived in Detroit, but didn't have the exact address. This was strange because during the interview he did not mention a sister. Thinking of who might be able to help, I went to my friend Matt's shop in Birmingham. Matt is good at digging up information on the Internet. With the assistance of his brother John, they came up with an address in Detroit. After leaving their shop, I entered the address into my GPS and headed out. I was uneasy about going to the house because it was in a bad area of Detroit. The traffic that afternoon was horrific, but eventually I found the address. It looked like someone lived in the home, but the window shades were pulled. There was no answer after knocking several times, so I went back to my car and started writing a note to stick on the front door. Then all of a sudden there was a tap on my car window. A fortyish looking man asked me what was going on. I told him the whole story and asked if the veteran's sister still lived there. He mentioned that the woman was his mother and that she died in 2012. Realizing that this guy was the veteran's nephew, I asked if he or someone else in the family could take care of his uncle. The nephew called his brother who agreed to pick the veteran up and take him home.

The next Monday I drove back to the nursing home and informed the veteran that his sister died in 2012, but found a nephew that would take him in. He told me to go find the case worker on the second floor and tell her that his nephew would be coming to pick him up. After conveying what was going on, she said in a stern voice, "You can't take him out of here." I asked, "Why not?" and she said, "Not only is he mentally ill, but with the IVs and heart monitor hooked up to him, he's too sick to move." At that point I came back with a much stronger tone. "I've been visiting him for over a year and know that he is on oxygen, but not once have I ever seen him hooked up to an IV or a heart monitor. Also, what makes you think you're a Psychiatrist and can make a diagnosis that this man is mentally ill?" Throwing her hands in the air she declared, "I have never had anyone talk to me that way." I shot back, "You're lucky it wasn't me that was locked up against my will for over a year." Then I asked to get her supervisor on the phone. The woman called her boss and handed the phone over to me. The supervisor and I had a quick discussion and it turned out that there was no problem other than the veteran had to be out in 30 days. I called the nephews that afternoon and told them to pick up their uncle. There was still a concern about the drugs and how he would come down from his addiction. I advised the nephews to contact the VFW for help in that matter. Let's hope everything worked out.

Notes

1. shmoop – we speak student, *The Wizard of Oz*, "We're not in Kansas anymore,"
https://www.shmoop.com/quotes/were-not-in-kansas-anymore.html

2. Gerber Life Insurance Company, "Gerber Grow-up Plan,"
https://www.gerberlife.com/child-life-insurance/grow-up-plan

3. Cindy Boren, September 26, 2016, The Washington Post, "The story behind how Arnold Palmer invented his famousdrink,"
https://www.washingtonpost.com/news/early-lead/wp/2016/09/26/the-story-behind-how-arnold-palmer-invented-his-famous-drink-the-arnold-palmer/?utm_term=.8c64c5370246

4. Medline Plus, Trusted Health Information for you, "Delirium Tremens,"
https://medlineplus.gov/ency/article/000766.htm

5. MDHHS, Michigan Department of Health and Human Services, "Health Care Coverage for Adults,"
http://www.michigan.gov/mdhhs/0,5885,7-339-71547_2943---,00.html

6. drugs.com, Know more. Be sure, "Fentanyl Injection,"
https://www.drugs.com/fentanyl.html

7. Frederick Dove, 3 November 2011, BBC News, "What's happened to Thalidomide babies?"
http://www.bbc.com/news/magazine-15536544

8. Esther Heerema, MSW, June 16, 2017, Very Well, "Cerebral (Brain) Atrophy,"
https://www.verywell.com/what-is-cerebral-brain-atrophy-98812

9. RxList, "Norco (hydrocodone bitartrate and acetaminophen),"
http://www.rxlist.com/norco-drug.htm

10. wikipedia.org, The Free Encyclopedia, "Section 8 (housing),"
https://en.wikipedia.org/wiki/Section_8_(housing)

11. Louisiana Sports Hall of Fame, "Eddie Robinson,"
http://www.lasportshall.com/inductees/coach/eddie-robinson/

12. Redskin – History, Greatest Redskins, "#28 Darrell Green Cornerback,"
http://www.redskins.com/team/history/70-greatest-redskins/darrell-green.html

13. schizophrenia.com, "Paranoid Schizophrenia,"
http://www.schizophrenia.com/szparanoid.htm

14. drugs.com, Know More. Be Sure, "Mescaline,"
https://www.drugs.com/illicit/mescaline.html

15. drugs.com, Know More. Be Sure, "LSD,"
https://www.drugs.com/illicit/lsd.html

16. Opacity, "Northville State Hospital,"
http://opacity.us/site194_northville_state_hospital.htm

17. drugs.com, Know More. Be Sure, "PCP (Phencyclidine),"
https://www.drugs.com/illicit/pcp.html

18. history.com, "1881, Shootout and the O.K. Coral,"
http://www.history.com/this-day-in-history/shootout-at-the-ok-corral

19. Graeme McMillan, December 13, 2014, Your Hollywood Reporter, "Krypton: A Brief History of Superman's Perpetually Doomed Home Planet,"
http://www.hollywoodreporter.com/heat-vision/krypton-a-brief-history-supermans-757172

20. drugs.com, Know More. Be Sure, "Vicodin,"
https://www.drugs.com/vicodin.html

21. MS - National Multiple Sclerosis Society, "What Is MS?"
http://www.nationalmssociety.org/What-is-MS

22. drugs.com, Know More. Be Sure, "Methadone,"
https://www.drugs.com/methadone.html

23. The Recovery Village, "Opiate Addiction,"
https://www.therecoveryvillage.com/opiate-addiction/#gref

24. history.com, "1961, The Bay of Pigs Invasion Begins,"
http://www.history.com/this-day-in-history/the-bay-of-pigs-invasion-begins

25. history.com, "Cuban Missile Crisis,"
http://www.history.com/topics/cold-war/cuban-missile-crisis

26. history.com, "1063, John F. Kennedy Assassinated,"
http://www.history.com/this-day-in-history/john-f-kennedy-assassinated

27. Crohn's and Colitis, "Understanding Crohn's Disease,"
https://www.crohnsandcolitis.com/crohns

28. Drugs.com, Know More. Be Sure, "Doxepin (Sinequan),"
https://www.drugs.com/mtm/doxepin-sinequan.html

29. drugs.com, Know More. Be Sure, "Oxycodene,"
https://www.drugs.com/misspellings/oxycodine.html

30. Mayo Clinic, "Shaken Baby Syndrome,"
http://www.mayoclinic.org/diseases-conditions/shaken-baby-syndrome/basics/symptoms/con-20034461

31. wikipedia.org, "Republican Party (United States),"
https://en.wikipedia.org/wiki/Republican_Party_(United_States)

32. whitehouse.gov, "Dwight D. Eisenhower,"
https://www.whitehouse.gov/1600/presidents/dwightdeisenhower

33. BBC History, "Heinrich Himmler (1900 - 1945),"
http://www.bbc.co.uk/history/historic_figures/himmler_heinrich.shtml

34. biography.com, "Adolf Hitler, Director, Military Leader (1889 -1945),"
https://www.biography.com/people/adolf-hitler-9340144

35. history.com, "Vietnam War,"
http://www.history.com/topics/vietnam-war

36. wikipedia.com, "William Harrell Nellis,"
https://en.wikipedia.org/wiki/William_Harrell_Nellis

37. whitehouse.gov, "Abraham Lincoln,"
https://www.whitehouse.gov/1600/presidents/abrahamlincoln

38. stanford.edu, "The Earth's Ionoshpere,"
http://solar-center.stanford.edu/SID/activities/ionosphere.html

39. history.com, "Oklahoma City bombing,"
http://www.history.com/topics/oklahoma-city-bombing

40. The U.S. Department of Housing and Urban Development,
https://www.hudexchange.info/resources/documents/2016-AHAR-Part-1.pdf

41. Centers of Disease Control and Prevention,
https://www.cdc.gov/nchs/data/databriefs/db162.htm

42. McKinley Law, Marriage and Divorce,
https://www.cdc.gov/nchs/fastats/marriage-divorce.htm

Other books by Celano family members:

Create Realistic Portraits with Colored Pencils

Triangulate Your Golf Swing

Golf: A Beginners Guide and Reference

Moving Beyond the Third Fret

Henrietta's Journal

Aunt Bobbie's Favorite Family Recipes

They Would be Gods: A Love Story

Available at Amazon.com and other online bookstores.